Is My Leading & Teaching Reaching?

__Is My Leading & Teaching Reaching?__ Is an educator's resource tool that will benefit both the administrator and classroom teacher as it answers the question, "What does my administrator observe, what is being noted, and what are the expectations during a walkthrough of my classroom?"

By William Montoya

Editor:	Elizabeth Palma
Front Cover Designer:	Margot Maurer
Back Cover Designer:	Robert King

ISBN: 978-1-938950-83-4
Publisher:
Greater Is He Publishing 9824
E. Washington St.
Chagrin Falls, Ohio 44023
Phone: 216.288.9315
GreaterIsHePublishing.com

Author:
Señor William Montoya
216 883-7374 Home
216 513-5064 Mobile
Monty1906@hotmail.com
William.Montoya@Clevelandmetroschools.org

CONTENTS

Dedicated To:

Dr. Barbara Schmidt-Rinehart my professor and mentor at Ashland University. You inspired me to always achieve what appeared to be the unachievable.

Brother William Martin my spec, middle school principal (boss), friend, and mentor. You took a chance on a spirited, zealous, and carefree student-teacher, teacher, coach, and administrator. You saw into my spirit and believed in me and my passion for kids. I miss your presence in my life like nobody's business.

Dr. Shirley Robinson my first elementary school principal (boss). You pushed me to places I didn't know I could go. Your faith in me to perform tasks and not be micromanaged, gave me self-esteem and confidence.

Christy Nickerson my high school principal (boss), friend and sister in Christ Jesus. You valued my work, protected my integrity, and allowed me to shine in areas where the darkness seemed to take over. I will always appreciate your small gestures of appreciation and worth. Being valued is the greatest gift you could give a classroom teacher. Your faith in me carried me through!

To all the spectacular teachers that I was blessed to observe, evaluate, and enjoy your lessons. You are the reason I wrote this book. I want the world to know that you, your work, and dedication to our babies is valued and honored. Your teaching strategies reached every student and no matter their circumstance you gave them the gift of an optimal education. I could discern that your hearts and your souls poured into your passion to teach. ¡Bravo and Ole to the teachers of Collinwood, Southview, Buhrer, and Walton! I won't state any names for fear that I will forget someone but I know you know EXACTLY who you are!

Preface

Can a teaching resource tool be written for educators that will withstand the ages, never be outdated and always be useful? A loaded question right? This is an attempt to create such a resource tool that speaks to the effective teaching approaches that will help any educator at any age in any era of their teaching or administrative career **REGARDLESS OF HOW MANY "NEW WAYS" OF PROFESSIONAL DEVELOPMENT AND TRAINING ARE CREATED!**

From a **teaching** lens how do I know if my teaching is reaching my students? Beyond the qualitative data, how can I effectively deliver instruction when every year (or in some cases every quarter) it seems my district is spear-heading, piloting, or implementing some "New and Innovative Research Based Initiative" which will supposedly "improve" leading, teaching, learning, and of course assessment scores?

From an **administrative** lens, do I possess the skill set to make an informed evaluation of my teachers? What am I (as the instructional leader of my school) observing and what do I note during a walkthrough of my schoolrooms? What are my expectations of teachers, students, and classrooms when I enter a lesson for a walkthrough?

This resource tool will offer **TEACHERS AND ADMINISTRATORS** a blueprint of effective tips, data collection and feedback styles, along with clear ideas of what is being noticed and the expectations that are desired during a walkthrough of a classroom lesson.

What makes me qualified to offer you such a tool? I have been blessed to have more than a quarter century in educational experience at the urban level.

My career began in Cleveland, Ohio as a high school substitute teacher at Collinwood High School in January of 1993. Later on that fall of 1993, in my first official teaching position at R.G. Jones Elementary School, I pioneered our district's first FLES School. In an attempt to offer Foreign Language in the Elementary School (FLES) as a "magnet" program, I was blessed to teach Spanish to **preschoolers through 5th grade.**

While earning a Master Degree in Administration at Kent State University, a Spanish position, volleyball and cheer position became available in the fall of 1998 at Collinwood Middle School. Reluctantly, I left my "babies" to teach 8th grade Spanish and coach high school volleyball and cheerleaders at Collinwood.

As a new **high school coach** and **middle school teacher**, my Collinwood cheer team earned a runner up and two cheer titles, while the volleyball team finished in the final four twice and earned a runner up in the city final. Here, I began developing rapport and a leadership skill set both on the court and in the classroom while experiencing the world of the middle school student.

Believing I could handle an administrative role and having faith in my abilities to lead, Mr. Martin (mentioned in the dedication) asked me to assume the position of **freshmen principal** after returning from the 1999 Winter Break.

In January of 2000 I inherited 402 freshmen including the 156 repeating freshmen from the prior school year. With 26 teachers, a secretary and school counselor, I was asked to "do your thing" and "enact some order" to the chaos the unit was causing due to the absence of their freshmen administrator (whom was out on sick leave the entire year). Once again, I warily left my kids (8th graders) and both athletic teams to serve in high school administration.

In 2003 I began my 2nd pioneering career as I traveled to Lorain, Ohio to help **convert two major comprehensive high schools into smaller learning communities.** I principled one of the seven small schools during Lorain's transitional era.

Later, in 2005-2006 I returned to Cleveland and embarked into the world of **elementary administration** at Buhrer School. Wearing the hat of **Dual Language Administrator,** I wrote a Foreign Language Assistance Program (FLAP) grant for a little over $750,000.00 to improve the newly birthed Dual Language Program at Buhrer. Three years later I returned to **middle school, not as a teacher but as an administrator** at Walton Bilingual School in Cleveland.

In 2010-2011 I set sail for home and arrived **back into the classroom** where I am presently teaching Spanish, Senior Seminar and serving as the volleyball coach, cheer coach, and senior class advisor at the home of the Mighty Golden Scarabs; East Technical High School, home of Olympic Heroes Jesse Owens and Harrison Dillard.

Located in the heart of urban Cleveland, East Tech is an identified poverty stricken high school where 100% of the students receive a free breakfast and lunch. The school is 98% African American, approximately 42% are "identified" as special education, the average 9th grader is reading at almost a fifth grade level (mean lexile 4.9). An October 2015 quarterly report showed that 48.4% of the students are reading proficient, 38.7% of the students are math proficient, 83.2% of the students attend school regularly, 86% of the students have committed a serious discipline event resulting in suspension which consequently hinder and prevent learning.

This report includes a survey called "Conditions for Learning" which speak to the Social and Emotional Learning of our Scarabs. This survey echoes that 83.8% of our students feel safe at school, 86.2% feel they have the support of the staff while 93.9% of the kids reaffirm the work they are doing in the classroom is challenging. In summary only 36.8% of the student body feel they are receiving adequate social and emotional learning. The demographics illustrates most of the students are being raised by a single mom or other female, as almost 91% of fathers are either in prison or absent from the home.

East Tech is considered a "poor performing high school" as identified by the Ohio Department of Education receiving an "D" rating with a performance index of 56.1%, and an "F" rating for state indicators met (2015). Tech is geographically positioned in Cleveland's largest public housing area with projects directly to the front, back, and either sides of the facility.

Despite the disparity our children face each day of their lives, they are fabulous children. I am proud to serve them and proud to say that while teaching them I was honored to <u>earn the highest rating;</u> "<u>Accomplished</u>" under the new Teacher Evaluation Development System (TDES) in 2013-2014.

Due to their success in my classroom I have been privileged to present **<u>at the National Teacher's Convention</u>** for High Schools That Work in Charlotte, North Carolina. I am fulfilled to say that I have presented this information in countless schools including my own, and schools that have invited me to present this "very useful" professional development tool.

My many blessings professionally come with **<u>being qualified</u>** in the Walkthrough Protocol by Carolyn Downey and the opportunity to work with and be **<u>trained by</u>** Margarita Calderon and Liliana Minaya-Rowe in the areas of developing and implementing a Two-Way Immersion Program, and a step by step protocol for integrating vocabulary and writing in all curriculums.

Despite all of my years' experience and training there is nothing more validating than when fellow educators share with me that my "blueprint" has not only helped them tremendously with teaching and learning, but has been valuable in preparing them for their evaluation. Colleagues have indicated they are performing at the highest levels of teaching, and that these strategies have all but **eliminated classroom management issues.** I pray that you will use this blueprint tool to do just that, enhance you as a professional and also increase your value as a respected, prepared, and knowledgeable educator of young people.

To that end I will make an attempt to explain and describe the classroom walkthrough from my administrative perspective. Why mine? Because when I decided to marry it, it completely changed the vibe of my building and my view of what is millennial education. This visitation process is designed to provide meaningful opportunities for both administrator and teacher to reflect and dialogue about instruction. This resource tool will act as a protocol **to gain valuable information** about critical aspects of the teaching-learning exchange, including objectives taught, teaching strategies, and student involvement.

For my book to be an effective utensil for teachers and principals, the process **must be repeated** constantly and consistently throughout the year especially in the 1st quarter. Because visits are short, repeated visits are necessary for participants **to develop a valid profile** of a specific classroom's efficacy. After many visits, patterns and commonalities emerge in both individual classrooms and in the entire building that can be used as topics for exploration through conversation, collaboration and critical thinking.

Ultimately, the goal is to move every employee to a comfort level with open and honest analysis of professional performance and with development of personal and professional growth responsibilities. Institutionalizing the practice of walkthroughs **away from conventional evaluations** to a collegial process will celebrate the interdependence of all educators.

Before we jump into the work with regards to the expectations from both teachers and administrators concerning walkthroughs, we have to agree that there are three commitments required to do this work as well as 10 strategies that must be adhered to when reflecting on the offstage classroom expectations that all educators should have in the forefront of teaching. These **three commitments and ten strategies** will set the foundations for the preparation of the walkthrough process. You must make a covenant with yourself in order to get the results you desire. Will you? Will you make that covenant for your upgrading and for the improvement of leading and teaching? Let us embark on a journey toward still waters and green pasture.

Chapter 1
PerCoDiff
100mg daily.

During a classroom walkthrough there are many things that are being noticed. A walkthrough is designed to help check for students' understanding and rigor in lesson plans, students' work and conversations. This resource compendium will also serve as a reflective teaching tool concerning classroom pedagogy and teaching practices. Will you **commit** to taking a daily dose of **PerCoDiff**, and live by the acronym **"Every Child Is Worthy and Safe"**?

I promise you will achieve levels of continuous improvement if you commit daily to:

- **Personalization**
- **Collaboration**
- **Differentiation (PerCoDiff) and believing (in)**
- **EVERY CHILD IS WORTHY AND SAFE:**
- **Engagement, Curriculum, Instruction, Walls of Students' Work and Safety.**

Here are some commitments, self-reflective statements, and essential questions to consider when taking your daily early morning dose of **PerCoDiff**...

The 1st daily commitment is to **personalize** with your students. Consider these questions when getting to "know" students:

➢ Do I sufficiently probe my students' knowledge, abilities, and processes? (I need to know my students well).

➢ Are the assessments I give them fair/appropriate for the levels of their abilities considering their gender, culture, and language aspects?

➢ Do my students see me as one whom appreciates them and enjoys working with them? Knowing my students personally does not mean becoming their "BFF".

The 2nd Daily Commitment is to **collaborate** with your colleagues. Consider these questions when collaborating with colleagues:

➢ Do I create horizontal and vertical instruction?

➢ My students <u>are</u> learning....but are they learning the right things?

➢ Am I referencing my district's Scope and Sequence Guide and the Common Core Quick Flip Reference Booklet to plan lessons?

➢ Do I discuss the hidden strengths of challenging students and the instructional strategies that best fit them with my colleagues?

➢ Do I discuss fair and appropriate assessment techniques for evaluating progress and for making instructional decisions with my colleagues?

> ➢ Am I communicating with support staff and other elective teachers to see how they can assist in the instruction of the content standards?

The 3rd Daily Commitment is to **differentiate** instruction in our classrooms so that 100% of the students are learning at their cognitive level. Consider these questions about differentiation:

> ➢ Do I whole group teach too much?
> ➢ Does my room have structure, organization, a sense that education is valued?
> ➢ Do I have safety nets in place to assist students who need additional time or help learning a concept?
> ➢ Am I aware of how culture and gender influence students' interaction and communication styles?
> ➢ Is my lesson organized so that I whole group teach, differentiate, and foster student talk through a share out time, review, and next steps?
> ➢ Do I utilize a variety of instructional strategies such as the Marzano 9* to help students achieve?

When you take a daily dose of **PerCoDiff** understand that its implications by default, establish a culture of high expectations. You will begin to reflect on your decisions and classroom practices. Prayerfully, you will be able to acknowledge whether you are an "enabler", "controller", or "nurturer" of young people.

Chapter 2
Talented
"10"...

There are **ten strategies** that I live by when thinking about how I desire for my classroom to feel to students when they cross the threshold of my room. I share these strategies with the intentions that you **follow** them to the letter or at minimum use them as a basis for creating a culture that **fits your** classroom personality.

1. **DEVELOP, COMMUNICATE, AND IMPLEMENT CLASSROOM MOTIVATION AND MANAGEMENT PLANS.**

2. **DEVELOP INSTRUCTIONAL PLANS THAT FACILITATE BELL-TO-BELL TEACHING.**

3. **CREATE CLASSROOM ORGANIZATION AND ARRANGEMENT THAT SPURS PRODUCTIVITY.**

4. **ESTABLISH HIGH EXPECTATIONS.**

5. **COMMUNICATE EXPECTATIONS TO STUDENTS AND PARENTS.**

6. **VIEW THE STUDENT AS A WORKER. IMPLEMENT INSTRUCTIONAL ACTIVITIES THAT ACTIVELY ENGAGE STUDENTS.**

7. **KEEP STUDENTS ON TARGET.**

8. **ENCOURAGE FREQUENT AND RELEVANT FEEDBACK THAT WORKS.**

9. **ESTABLISH GRADING PRACTICES THAT COMMUNICATE HIGH EXPECTATIONS AND DECREASE FRUSTRATION.**

10. **IMMEDIATELY DEAL WITH BEHAVIOR OUT OF ESTABLISHED NORMS.**

**The 1st strategy** will assure that acceptable student behavior and day-to-day operation of your classroom ensues. To be more productive and focused these plans should be posted in the room as norms and discussed and re-visited at minimum once or twice a month. When I transitioned back to high school, I discovered that my motivational and management plans were called a syllabus. Of course the word "syllabus" was used in college to outline the expectations of the work I would be doing all semester. This is also true for students who require structure.

It is to your benefit as well as theirs to understand what it is they will learn when they will learn it, and the assignments they are expected to complete. Students become active partners with you in what they learn when they know exactly what it is for which they are accountable.

These plans can be yearlong (which I do not like) or they can be done by semester, or quarterly.

In my district (and hopefully yours) there is a "Scope and Sequence" and a "Pacing" guide which detail specifically what standards to teacher early in each quarter and late in each quarter. These assets keep me accountable to remain on track and teach what I am supposed to teach. Prayerfully, your guides are congruent to your state standards (or common core) so that you are not only teaching, **but teaching the "right stuff".**

Any educator that assumes children "know how to act" is setting themselves up for failure! Your precise expectations should be posted. They should all begin positively and stated clearly; "**Students will**….." I have seen posters of rules that begin with, "Students will not…." and it makes for a poor climate. Students will become literal with you about your "do not(s)" and will police them to the ultimate letter. Don't set yourself up.

Be careful to post management plans, expectations, rubrics, and protocols on your walls as decorations. These guidelines should be living breathing artifacts you and your students abide by every day. These plans become more effective when you review them orally and in writing with students and parents. The vital goal is that everyone is on the same page and no one can say to you, "I didn't know that". If you are savvy, you will include your students in the creation of your classroom norms. Norms are exactly what it means; the "normality" of your classroom.

Always keep in mind that <u>Policies</u> are school-wide expectations, <u>Rules</u> are few and never changing, while <u>Procedure</u> is uniquely your preference as to what constitutes **"business as usual"** in your classroom.

Student performance and academic standards posters should be motivational. Incorporating your mascot into your academic standards is one of the best ideas I have ever posted in my room. Students earning D's are recognized as "Scarabs on the Move"; those earning C's I say are, "Scarabs on Track"; those earning B's are referred to as "Scarabs Reaching for the Top" and those earnings A's are deemed "Mighty Elite Scarabs......WHAT!"

Your consequences and rewards should be outlined clearly. Students who know what will happen to them when they violate the norms of the room are not likely to commit infractions. Your plan should also state what happens to students who meet and exceed the norms. I have a three tier hierarchy of consequences that works well and took years to refine.

When a norm gets violated I have a **<u>recuperative conversation</u>** which is no more – no less than a whisper in the ear or a conversation away from others. I never put any of my students on blast as I am well aware that I will exacerbate the unwanted behavior and/or open myself up for an ugly confrontation. My second tier is a **<u>spoken warning</u>**. "Tyrone, I have spoken to you about your disruption, consider this is your warning". Usually the death stare or look gets them back in line as well as close proximity and/or a touch on the shoulder.

I cannot recall the last time I reached tier three which was to **call home** or write an **office referral**. Because of PerCoDiff, I almost never have any classroom management issues; my students know me, what my agenda is, and what lines not to cross. That is the culture I have established!

      Your plan should include safety nets. The reoccurring theme in my classroom is high expectations. "**I am preparing you for the next level**" is a sentence my students hear every time I hear grumbling in the air. I balance this theme with a clear message that I am always available to assist anyone having or requiring assistance. Students who are falling off or are struggling with challenging assignments need to know that you are willing to help them to develop productive learning habits. The plan should include when, where, and how students can get support and how and what *they* must do to get it. My room is open at lunch (despite that my contract states I am entitled to an uninterrupted lunch) to safety net students (mostly athletes) who need to catch or make up work. This **lunch bunch** time is also used to help students one on one.

      Genuine three-way communication is wanted, expected and necessary. Your plan needs to clearly state how you will communicate with parents, students and yourself. They must understand that in order for everyone to succeed, there must be away to get a hold of each other. In this new era of social media and technology, there is **NO WAY** a parent; student and teacher should not communicate.

Email addresses and phone numbers should be in your plan as well as user names and passwords for parents to utilize if your district (like mine) expects you to use an electronic grade book such as <u>Engrade</u>. Most vendors who sell electronic grade book licenses have a manner in which they assign the student their own username and password as well as the parent. Fortunately for me, parents can email me on Engrade to inform, ask, or clarify any issues they are experiencing with their child.

This 1st strategy is paramount in the first week of school. When you set the tone by making your motivational and management plans livable-breathable documents, you will see a drastic improvement in your classroom culture. Don't forget to take your daily dose of <u>PerCoDiff</u> and refer to your plans once or twice a week. Stick to your guns and never deviate. You don't want students thinking you are a push over, inconsistent, or able to be manipulated. There is clear line you should develop with your babies; a line they should know never to cross.

Chapter 3
Saved
By the
Bell

The 2nd strategy is your ability to empower the bell (or in my case the long beep sound) system as a clear trigger to get down to business. The other component is to make certain that you have developed on optimal lesson plan. The dual goal of this strategy is to maximize your teaching time and communicate high expectations for on-task behavior. The bottom line for me has always been this fact; I have 180 days to teach a curriculum that I am accountable for and that students will need to be prepared for the next level of learning!

Having bell to bell engagement is critical to establishing effective procedure. Essential techniques for achieving 100% student participation should be evident as the students are walking toward your classroom. They should see you standing **at the door** ready to greet them and give them detailed directions. Even before a pinky toe enters my room, students know what **voice level is appropriate** and what the **expectation is**. In my case, "In a restaurant voice volume, please get your notebook out of the crate and begin doing your "Bell Ringer" (bell work)." Visible to them upon entering the room is the **Day's Objective**, the **Bell Ringer**, and the **Exit Ticket** for the lesson. There is no time to waste. The moment they enter your classroom they know it is time to get down to business.

Once **Bell Ringers** are collected (or spot checked) the <u>transition to the lesson should be smooth</u>. Again, students should be given precise instructions before anyone moves and waiting for you to tell them to go ahead and accomplish the directive you give them. I have learned over the years that a very effective strategy is to **immediately highlight** those two or three students who are doing exactly what you have directed; ("Devonte and Chira have their notebooks out and pencil ready".) This narrating technique not only repeats the direction to your babies but also will trigger those not doing what you ask to get with the program and indirectly gives them another chance to get on task!

Your lesson plan should include **five learning segments** and a summary activity after each segment. In my case the **first segment** is my Bell Ringer. This segment *links the day's objective* to previous lessons or homework. The data collected in the Bell Ringer always drives what I should re-teach (if necessary) or informs me of the students who have mastered or are close to mastering the standard at hand. The **second segment** is my direct instruction to clarify, review or introduce new material. During this "I-do" segment or whole class instruction, I am modeling the expectations I desire while constantly doing *formative assessments* (like thumbs up or thumbs down) to make certain everyone understands.

The **third segment** is the "We-do" portion where I am conveying knowledge through *differentiating instruction* and *scaffolding techniques*. These student centers keep students accountable for their work and allow some level of engagement between me and those who are working together. In some cases this "noise" in the room may appear chaotic, but it is healthy noise.

The **fourth segment** is the "You-do" or "Do it alone" portion of the lesson where I walk about facilitating the learning environment while students are on auto-pilot. This is the pinnacle time for me because it allows me to really see who is guessing, who almost gets it and who is confident about their work and answers.

The **fifth segment** is the Exit Ticket (usually signaled by the sound of my mobile phone which I have programmed to sound 5 minutes before the end of the period). This acts as *a summary- reflection of the lesson, and/or mastery check,* of the skill I wanted them to learn, or a link to the next day's lesson.

Bell to bell instruction is the absolute key to eradicating behavior problems. There is no time for foolishness when young people understand you have a procedure and that there is no time for lollygagging or tomfoolery. Coupled with the fact that you are placing a **point value** to the activities of the lesson plan into your electronic grade book, students will begin to understand that in order to achieve the desired mark, they are accountable for their work and how it gets completed.

Engrade (for me) is a Godsend. It allows me to assign a percent value to Exams, Notebook, Participation, Attendance, and Homework.
Once I enter the assignment and assign it a point value, it begins tabulating students' percent from day one!
There is no ambiguity!

The shift of accountability is in the hands of my kids! I am constantly pointing at my "Academic Standard" poster while reminding them how to achieve "Mighty Elite Scarab", status. You are beginning to build **an enormous bridge** with them where now accountability is the deciding factor for the desired mark in your classroom and in your course.

Chapter 4

No mess

No stress

The 3rd strategy speaks to student productivity and teacher effectiveness. If productivity and effectiveness are areas you can improve, while maintaining classroom management, make certain the space (your classroom) you are blessed with is not a hot mess. I have been in classrooms where cardboard boxes are piled in corners and on filing cabinets, graded and half graded student artifacts were all over the place, and where posters hanging on the walls were older than Methuselah.

A room with no strategic sense of organization concerning furnishings, materials or equipment will compromise the climate and "feel of your room". Optimal learning and teaching cannot come to fruition in the midst of chaos and junk. Disorganization is not beneficial to teaching or learning and will absolutely **cause unwanted stress in your students**. Some students (like mine) may use your mess against you and blame you for "that lost test" that was allegedly completed and submitted on time.

Most of the time students need motivation, wellness and a good attitude to consider learning what you desire them "to get". My years of experience has informed me that in order to get them remotely close to the **"desire phenomenon"** (an intrinsic desire to learn), you must do all you can to favorably impact their senses. Make sure they see rich color in your room, get rid of faded posters! Bite the bullet and purchase new, rich in print and colorful artifacts for your walls.

Personalize the space they touch. You should always try to increase face-to-face engagement. Always **work toward a cooperative setting** where think pair share is evident (two desk together), quads (four desks together), tables of students, or a "U" shaped arrangement where you know students can see the faces of those that are speaking, learning, and participating. I love the "U" shaped configuration because it allows me to circulate into the space of learners (and yes, distracters) within a few steps.

If ever I learned a lesson while teaching was to, at no time, begin using my room as a storage space. Like clothing, if it hasn't been used in a year, discard it or give it away! Students and visitors should not see boxes and piles of "stuff" crammed in the corners or piled high on furnishings.

Storing materials at pick up points accessible to students cuts down on wasted time. Establishing a protocol as to where to drop off homework or completed work (In Box) and picking up graded papers (Out Box) will minimize distractions and clutter. Have several garbage cans in your room in different corners and **do not** make your desk the focal point.

In my professional opinion, lining up desks like head stones in a cemetery with the teacher desk in the middle is traditional and the **worst arrangement**. Here are some questions to consider when you are thinking about strategy three:

- ✓ **Is my space inviting or not?**
- ✓ **Is my room colorful?**
- ✓ **Is my room soothing?**
- ✓ **Is my room neat?**
- ✓ **Is my room focused?**
- ✓ **Does my room inspire quality student work?**
- ✓ **Does my room diminish noise and confusion?**
- ✓ **Does my room arrangement allow students to hide and opt out of student engagement?**

Kids are dealing with enough stress as it is! Adding to their stress only compounds the concerns and worries they already feel about being academically successful. When students are engrossed in sponge activities, tests, silent readings and self-practices, the use of low volume music is also comforting. Playing music has also served as **an effective device** for their sense of hearing. Hearing music can be a cue to get down to business. Or when it is turned off, a cue to stop and pause for precise directions. How then, is using music, beneficial to class climate? Because when used effectively it can establish a norm of focus and an environment that communicates high expectations **for starting and completing tasks** in a timely manner!

Chapter 5

"Am I getting

an A?"

One of the things I have come to respect from all my students is their candidness about grades. Those that just want to know clearly how to earn an A in my class simply want you to tell them how to earn it. ___The 4th strategy___ addresses academic expectations and what you can do to answer the question, "How do I get an A+ in here?"

In the 1st strategy I mentioned that student performance and academic standards posters should be motivational. Tied to this, should be a rubric for each project, assessment, PBL, or activity, which is assigned a point value and thus a grade. All too often I have made the mistake of teaching multitudes of **"pieces parts"** and doing a poor job at providing my students with a way to internalize how the parts fit together into **a meaningful whole.** So what I began doing was giving them clear and concise rubrics and criteria for earning the preferred grade.

Like Grant Wiggins in his <u>backward</u> design, I learned to avoid arguments with students and parents about grades by teaching and assessing with the <u>end</u> in mind.

Some techniques I have used to entice high expectations are to:

- **Show some examples or models of completed works or projects**
- **In math, show students of well thought-out solutions to math problems, and good solution methods**
- **In music, letting students listen to a recording of an orchestra playing a new piece of music before sight-reading the music for the first time**
- **In computer tech, showing a video of the insides of laptop before teaching about the individual parts**
- **In ELA, passing out a well written essay and reviewing its contents before asking them to write one**
- **In Spanish Class, watching a video of salsa, cumbia, merengue, and bachata dancing before teaching them to dance each of them.**

Rubrics and/or criteria will stress the importance of learning everything you are teaching them. Your formative (and traditional) assessment of A, B, C, D, and F grades will communicate volumes if you change your **"F" to "NY"** (not yet) and your **"0" points earned to "M"** (missing work). Children have (privately) expressed to me that seeing an "F" or a "0" on Engrade (or on a graded assignment), is interpreted or insinuates, "Don't ask! This is not up for discussion! "

Don't except "F" work or "0" points earned, from your students. Consider allowing your students a window of time to get themselves together…..Please!

Establishing High Expectations has proven to be most challenging for me when it comes to teaching in urban America. It's a daily struggle, a period to period tussle. The world most of my students live in each day is compounded by the "adult" challenges they should not have to face until they are adults. Unfortunately, outside of the confines of East Tech, hunger, drugs, violence, family dysfunction, gang war fare, shootings, being robbed at gun point, dealing drugs, stealing, or walking on the safe side of East 55th Street to stay alive, is their priority not English, Math, Science, History or for that matter how to say, "May I use the restroom?", in Spanish. They **are in survival mode** all day every day.

The existential plights they face on a day to day basis far outweighs my lesson objective for the day. Therefore, finding that middle ground where I can maintain my teaching integrity while being cognizant of their world; **and** maintain high expectations, is extremely challenging. This is why the **Per** in my daily dose of **PerCoDiff** is so imperative. Without Personalization, they will simply shut down on me. My kids aren't stupid they know exactly what teachers have a vested interest in them and what teachers don't. When they know you love them, they will work like soldiers for you regardless of their situation. **Why? Because you are ALL THEY HAVE.**

How will you find this middle ground? Get to know them. Talk to them outside of the classroom. Attend a game or activity they participate in and yell out their name. Tell them you love them on Friday afternoon when the last bell sounds. My standing in the hallway imploring them to stay out of weekend drama and come back safely to me on Monday morning is a huge deal to my babies. Believe me when I tell you, **you're making a connection**, like Darquill waiting by the door after class stating, "You not going say it Señor?" and me replying, "Oh right…Diós los bendiga a todos, love yal, have a safe evening".

Chapter 6

I'm telling

your mom!

In strategy one I asked you to consider a three-way communication plan that identifies specifically how you, the student, and parent will connect when needed. *The 5th strategy* of communicating expectations to students and parents is a bit different.

This strategy will specifically and in detail explain and describe how the parent and the student become active partners in the responsibility **for producing quality, age appropriate, and grade level appropriate work.** The parents and guardians I deal with on a daily basis just want to know, "How is Kija doing in your class?" Which now bears the question; do I give her the letter grade Kija is earning? Or do I explain and go into depth a bunch of percentages she doesn't care to hear and/or won't understand? How do I communicate how Kija is doing and what she needs to do to produce quality work?

Because (as stated previously) Engrade is a computer assisted management of my grading, I am able to keep daily records of assignments and thus have the possibility of keeping parents informed on a daily basis. No student (or parent) likes surprises or being blindsided when it comes to less than acceptable performance. So the transference of responsibility now lies in the lap of student and parent.

In my humblest opinion (and probably in 100% of educators) it's easier for a parent to contact me about their (one) child than for me to contact all of my 150+ parent(s) or guardian(s). There is no time in the work day to make these voluminous phone calls.

When it came to understanding why some of the educators I observed were more effective than others (when it came to effective home communication), I discovered that my effective teachers, rather than admonishing parents for *not* helping students with out of class work, they **provided their parents with weekly reports** and expected their parents to **sign off** on homework, encouraged proofreading, and in some cases when possible, expected parents to tutor difficult content when possible.

When introducing the chapter on the American-Indian War, Miss Capello encouraged her parents to take their youngster to see (now rent) "Dances With Wolves". Miss Kureck encouraged her parents to sign off on Winter Break packets and stated that a 100% return with parent signatures and a (working) phone number would result in a **return from break pizza party**. Weekly reports of Carl doing his work in all his classes kept him eligible for football season and consequently being eligible for the team's MVP award.

This hue of communication, balanced with sufficient in class supervision and assessment of what students can produce independently, **re-affirms the team approach** to learning and alleviates the surprise or "gotcha" factors associated with totally teacher owned assessment of how students are performing.

Writing personal notes in <u>Engrade</u> next to the student's name rather it be, "Markell needs to practice conjugation of –ir verbs", or " Shadejza didn't complete her test because she went home ill", is an effective tactic I use to remind me of things and to inform parents of needed improvements or praise reports of their child.

Requiring parent participation and sharing expectations in advance, clearly communicates high expectations to all parties and allows them the satisfaction of a job well done. **Don't get jammed** with unwanted and unnecessary parent, teacher tiffs about grades and marks. Be clear, be very clear!

Chapter 7

Motivating millennials.

Do you know why Yonnie and Arsuntae spend countless hours in the gym playing basketball while Drew and Tyree can't get enough of their "NBA 2K" game on their Play Station? Or why students love playing different games on their tablets and cell phones? It is because of **two** points I have identified over the years of teaching and observing. Today's students are personally interested and only involved in things that produce **clear results** and are **interesting to them**. What a great motivational catalyst to possess if you are trying to educate millennials! **_Strategy 6_** is the best tool to develop to ensure that 100% of your students are actively engaged in your classroom.

The children above were great students in my classroom and on the court. I enjoyed watching them play and practice. Several times I observed them on the court and noticed they were **not worried** about perhaps being injured. They intently listened to Coach Brett or Coach Melvin while thinking, and risking their bodies to execute plays that possibly could have caused them hurt. I wondered; how could I transfer and produce such **clear and positive results** in the classroom as both coaches did on the basketball court?

Was I being a hypocrite or being labeled "a boring teacher" when I relied on only instructional planners to produce clear positive results? My students seemed uninterested in learning and the majority of my classroom time was passive with **me in control** and onstage. I was holding students hostage and making them accountable for their performance without really giving them an opportunity to perform.

I began to discover that the direct relationship between what was completed in my lessons and what was expected on Friday tests were vague to my babies and making them resent me and the test. When I finally got up enough courage to ask them if they enjoyed my class, they (bluntly and directly) expressed that they **only** enjoyed my class on the days when they had **opportunities to express** and produce their thoughts either on paper, in discussion, or on projects. When I asked them what kind of adjustments they thought I could make, these are some of the things they asked me to consider:

1. **Ask us thoughtful questions.**
2. **Require us to think for ourselves.**
3. **Listen (not hear) to what we have to say.**
4. **Value the questions we have more than the answers you require.**
5. **Value what we think more than what you want us to think or say.**

I was shocked and humbled by their forthrightness but more intrigued that they wanted me to value them as human, thinking, young adults.....wow!

I found myself making drastic changes in pedagogy as I began to focus on:

1. More than one page of writing each week. I planned for it and expected it!
2. Reading with students and sometimes to them.
3. Assigning reading primarily for homework.
4. Using more resources than just the textbook.
5. Requiring group or individual projects (PBL's) that would enhance their time management skills, planning skills, and communication skills, along with content mastery.

I had to accept that the "traditional" approach to teaching students **was long departed**. In a world of social media, where students are inundated with so much technology, I had to make adjustments and "keep up" with sign of the time.

I knew that if I wanted to make certain all kids were engaged, I had to contemplate their suggestions and make them feel esteemed as active workers in my classroom. Boy was this difficult for me because I now had the commission of implementing relevant instructional strategies on their level **not my own**. Thank goodness I had the privilege to read and meet Robert Marzano who wrote a life changing book on instructional strategies that aided me tremendously in crafting such plans. Later in the book, I will share with you these strategies and why they are considered the most effective stratagems to utilize in your classroom.

At the end of the day, it is unacceptable for less than 100% engagement of the students on your class list.

Granted there are circumstances where I am mindful that Deshawn is not having a good day, or that Adly is besieged with some personal issue she is having at home, but again, since I have personalized with my students, I am able to gently consider sensitive issues with "not being on task" and ask them to deliberate "letting it go" for the moment. This requires the gift of discernment. But this gift is only manifested if you have a vested interest in the lives of your students.....period!

There is a fine line between enabling students and allowing them "to put their head down" or having the moral courage to say, "I know what you are going through, do you wanna talk about it after class is over?" Believe me, when children know you are a heart with ears, they will situate their drama on hold and do what they have to **not because** they are scared of getting an "F for the day", but because they respect you enough to do the work that you are expecting them to complete. There is a difference. A huge difference! You have to be the one **who holds it together** for their benefit and yours.

Chapter 8

You promote

What you permit!

The 6th and 7th strategies go hand in hand. As previously discussed with strategy 6 where we began looking at students from a "student as worker" perspective and implementing activities that actively engage students, we are now faced with thinking about **keeping them on task** which is different from being engaged.

<u>***The 7th Strategy***</u> forced me to reflect on two behaviors that positively impacted my student's achievement. The first behavior was the **quality** of homework assignments **(by me)** and secondly, insisting that the work they handed in was not only **quality** work **(by them)**, but also congruent to their cognitive ability *and* on a higher level of Bloom's other than remembering and understanding.

As aforementioned, my Scarabs are very translucent and will shamelessly express themselves when given an opportunity. When asked, "Why did only 5 of you do the homework?" the overwhelming response (that day) was that they deemed the assignment **uninteresting and with little value** to their frame of reference or grade. Those that did complete the homework turned it in with very little care for presentation or neatness.

The quality was poor, unprofessional and quickly put together. When inadequate work was allowed to be turned in, I began to notice how my darlings would perpetually slap something on paper just to have something to turn in. Again I began dealing with this **perceived dilemma** that homework was not important and in no need of worth. Should I give up on homework or continue feeling frustrated?

My years of teaching has, if anything, taught me that students clearly know when you are assigning work that consists of **repeated skills, drills**, and thus overkill! I was forced to think about assignments that facilitated the learning necessary to attain required knowledge for the next day's lesson rather than giving homework that could **potentially be harmful to learning**. Why harmful? Because for the student population that I am blessed to teach, resources required to complete homework are very limited, out of reach, and time consuming. Homework is doomed from the start.

Due to this epiphany on the whole topic of its value, I began, (and so should you), thinking of homework as an **activity they needed to build on tomorrow's lesson**. This tactic has enabled students to see a clear relationship between what they are asked to do outside of class and their opportunity to be successful in class tomorrow. Here are some ways I began **tying** homework to graded sponge activities:

1. **Reading**
2. **Taking notes**
3. **Outlining**
4. **Developing questions about the main points in the reading.**
5. **Finding examples of .....**

6. Using common elements at home to illustrate.
7. Writing and allowing students to personalize homework.
8. Short activities like 4 problems instead of 40 are just as meaningful and appreciated by families.
9. And as mentioned in strategy 5 asking parents to sign and review the homework.
10. Lastly, look at the work! If kids feel homework is not being graded or looked at, THEY WILL STOP doing it.

I began to be okay with **smaller quantities** of quality work **over** reams of mediocre work.

When asked to teach senior seminar, I realized that although it was a semester course and considered a "bird course", for many seniors, this was probably the most important class to develop a skill set they would need to be successful in post-secondary life. Allowing and planning class time for students to **proof read** and contribute **feedback on the work of peers**, was one way I improved the quality of what I read and graded.

Showing my seniors samples of quality (student generated) work from other classes or outside the classroom **encouraged confidence** in producing levels of work appropriate to each senior's abilities. It was a transformation of Coach Brett and Coach Mel from the court into the classroom. Writing with students ("I write-You write"), sharing teacher writing, reading with students, discussing teacher interpretation (what I saw), and thinking out loud with students, are **ways to model** "thinking", reinforce positive efforts, and increase the likelihood of quality work being produced and handed in.

When considering assignments that are interesting and of value to your students you may want to ponder the *Interpersonal* strategy of Silver, Strong and Perini's The Strategic Teacher. This strategy is one of five which foster students' need to relate personally to the curriculum and to each other. The **interpersonal strategy** is my favorite because it uses teams, partnerships, and coaching to motivate children through their drive for membership and relationships.

When forming partnerships is my goal for a lesson plan or project I use the **reciprocal learning strategy** which focuses on building partnerships between you and the students by me modeling teaching and learning, and by the students processing, predicting, questioning, clarifying, and summarizing what quality work looks like. Reciprocal learning and teaching **works toward builds gaps** in what is relevant and what is not as well as what quality work is and what quality work is not.

Chapter 9

Risky

feedback

Does taking risks frighten you? Would you rather play it safe? Is asking for feedback a sign that you are not certain of what you are doing? Would you rather just figure things out on your own? If the answers are an honest yes, you are not alone. The *8th Strategy* will help you (I pray) not to feel so insecure about the types of **decisions you are making** in the classroom despite how risky they are.

I used to think that asking for feedback would be interpreted as weakness and that my colleagues and administrators would appraise me poorly if I appeared to be uncertain about my teaching practices and methods. So rather than to risk the embarrassment I began building my lesson repertoire by simply continuing to do what worked and **stop doing** what did not work.

I felt alone because I desired feedback but was fearful to ask for it. In my opinion, being human requires positive feedback (from someone) when attempting to do new and innovative things especially with today's expertise with social media. Despite that I felt alone and anticipated positive affirmation for great lessons, I longed for safety net suggestions to help cushion bombed lessons. So instead of seeking adult feedback, I pointed to my kids.

I began noticing that the safety nets I was creating were a direct result of the criticism I was attaining from those lives I was teaching.

When I procured positive steps to engage my students more actively in learning, it became my responsibility to provide feedback that guided them through new learning experiences. When the learning experience failed to come to fruition I'd ask myself and them, "What could I have done better?"

In 2014 after finishing the unit, "¡A Comer!, I noticed that my students were not performing well on their' final test. They struggled with acquiring the highest available points on their vocabulary, speaking, and grammar rubrics. They suggested we visit a Latino restaurant to be assessed on the communication between each other and their server. After much deliberation and preparation I made reservations to pay "El Rincón Criollo", a Puerto Rican restaurant, a visit on the west side of Cleveland. I arranged and spoke to the manager about bringing a group of students as a cultural field trip and unit examination

Rather than to re-administer a written assessment, or make a feeble attempt to re-create a restaurant setting in my classroom, I escorted them to an authentic setting and administered their test based on the basic interpersonal communications skills they learned in class. I prepared the owner and the waitress with a set of questions and dialogue they should use with my students and prayed things went well. This would be a testimony to see if they "mastered" the chapter standards and if they could activate some higher level Bloom's to get through the experience. Risky? Absolutely! But a great capstone activity to culminate a unit and a great cultural experience for my babies, it was. This is now a yearly event for me, the students, and the restaurant. A much anticipated event.

Teachers must exploit new strategies (even if they are risky) to nurture and trigger students' higher order thinking as they construct meaning and knowledge. I hope you consider using some of these approaches which helped me tremendously develop my students' ability to apply, analyze, evaluate, and create new thinking:

- ✓ **Use effective questioning feedback techniques to keep students focused and directed.**
- ✓ **Begin and end every instructional segment with a review of yesterday's learning and the big picture.**
- ✓ **Inspire students to probe "why?" and "how do you know what you know?"**
- ✓ **Require your babies to express their thinking and learning through speaking, writing, and designing new solutions (preferably through an interactive notebook).**

Not only will doing these things result in higher student achievement, it will **bolster students' abilities** to retain and apply information.

When you encourage **constant,** frequent and relevant feedback that works, your scholars' voices are being heard and they initiate how well they are performing in relation to the standards they are expected to master. You are *"responding to the learner in terms of learning."* If you stay true to this plan, you will activate a new form of habit that not only focuses on what is important to learn, but offers an opportunity for you to praise even small steps of performances **that loose quality work**! You will then break the bad habit of habitually being negative about the things they did wrong, poorly, in error, and/or not done correctly. If you have brusque students like I do, THEY WILL let you know that your feedback is appreciated and anticipated.

Feedback is a two-way proposition, students should be given opportunities to give feedback on the quality and effectiveness of assignments and how they would prefer to receive help, **participate in the learning and help construct the learning process.** If you are like me, I always express to my students, "Ok y'all, we are going to try something risky, so if it works; wonderful! If it doesn't, we will not do it anymore, deal? ". Yet again my decisive goal was to encourage frequent and relevant feedback that works even if it required **a leap of faith.**

Chapter 10

Ball's in

your court.

Earlier in Chapter 5 I touched on the million dollar question most students want to know; "Am I getting a good grade?" While the 4th strategy addressed establishing high expectations the **_9th Strategy_** is geared toward establishing grading practices that reduce and decrease frustration.

When I began to teach at East Tech something powerful stood out for me when it came to student work. My students didn't think there was anything wrong with handing in work in pencil, scratched offs, folded into 8 squares, straight out of a pant pocket, or stained with grease or Kool-Aid splashes. Initially I'd instantly "feel some type of way" that they thought it would be acceptable to hand in work in those conditions. But I had to recess and again deliberate …

I realized after a year **that they simply had no reference frame** to recognize what was acceptable and what acceptable work wasn't. So I began to present them with acceptable forms of **work samples** that met high rubric criteria, average rubric criteria, and poor rubric criteria. Teachable moments like this allowed kinesthetic and visual learners to actually see, feel, and understand the desired work and why their work may have earned a mark of **NY.**

My babies needed scoring guides, rubrics, and criteria that clearly delineated what the expectations were for earning top grades (A's B's); acceptable grades (C's); and **Not Yet! (NY)** grades for work deemed by me to be unacceptable.

Here is the bottom line for increasing high expectations and reducing frustration (mine and theirs); I had to be **absolutely clear** when communicating student achievement and progress to students and parents!

This, in my professional opinion, has always been the most misused, misunderstood, and mistrusted issues in public schooling. Why? Because most parents that I have talked with all resoundingly say the same thing, "I don't understand her grading policy. I don't know what my child is supposed to know in her class, what my child is able to do, or what she wants from my child!" If you are a new teacher to the profession or a seasoned teacher that has dealt with this frustration re-read strategy 4 and reflect on the rubrics and criteria you are providing in your syllabus, on your room posters, or on the expectations of an assignment you are giving.

Lastly, ponder long and hard about the assessment(s) you are administering for a project, presentation, homework, in class assignment, writing, reading, worksheet (student artifact) or whatever the assignment you are giving. Ask yourself, "Will this assessment **reflect what my students are capable** of doing? Expected to do? And Produce acceptable work?

Do not enable students by accepting sub-standard work. Mark it "NY" and hand it back until they come see you for direction, clarification, & advice and do not accept it until it meets (minimally) the lowest points on the criteria you have set.

Sticking to your guns on this issue embraces the conviction that all students can and will learn. You will discover that responsibility for grades earned, will transition from your red ink pen to the student's choices and degree of effort. Don't you think you deserve the decrease in frustration? I did! It is easier at times to look at the hole students have dug themselves in and throw in the towel. Take a moment to **see the other side of the canyon** despite that the bridge to get there is raggedy or appears impossible to cross.

Chapter 11

Not

in here!

I had to leave this next strategy for last so that you don't think for a moment any of the aforementioned tactics were easy to come by, implement or activate in my more than two decades of daily routine. Most took months, semesters, if not years to develop. The joy in sharing their success with you is to help you avoid having to wait so long to make teaching your occupation and your vocation. The _10th Strategy_ centers on dealing with severe behavior.

Long gone are the years where it was enough for you to simply manage your students and keep them away from the office or the disciplinarian. When I began teaching in the early 90's if you could govern your students and **didn't write referrals, you were considered a "good teacher"**. Because controlling students has never been an issue of mine, I always assumed my colleagues were effectively handling theirs as well. It wasn't until I became an administrator that I started to discover who was teaching _and_ managing behavior vs. who wasn't teaching but managed behavior.

Severe behavior issues are evident and real in ALL schools. However, in urban schools such as Tech where children lack structure, stable homes, mentors, and role models, severe behavior and disruption is more prevalent.

Inevitably, even when all best practices are applied, there will be occurrences when students will exhibit behaviors **that must be dealt with in some overtly proactive manner**. "Talking the Talk" and "Walking the Walk", require that any behavior that destroys an atmosphere of common decency and safety must be addressed…publicly and privately!

As you begin to unfold this resource guide, you will understand that all of its content has a common fabric. The strategies, if put to use, will all but **eliminate severe behavior** or will aid in detouring it while you are doing what you are paid for …..To teach!

That common fabric; to be clear about everything and vague about nothing! I believe that these 7 guidelines have helped me to decrease the likelihood of tomfoolery, inappropriateness, foolishness, disrespect, or unwanted disruptions:

1. **Have clearly defined policies**
2. **Include ALL stakeholders in the development of those policies**
3. **Once is not enough; communicate your policies and consequences on a regular basis**
4. **Be proactive by having situational awareness of your room. When actions appear minor, but have the potential of inciting more serious behavior, NIP them in the bud! Don't wait! Don't allow "hot boxes" like inappropriate joking around, profanity, the "n" word (which is a daily battle even for me), gossiping, or bullying of any kind, to manifest.**

5. Apply consequences no matter who is the violator.
6. Never destroy an offender, publically shame them, or de-humanize them. Keep in mind that consequences are created to stop the undesired activity and teach more constructive behavior.
7. Build and maintain close relationships with your students.

If you have attempted to handle your severe behaviors and have exhausted all means possible, there is nothing wrong with considering the consequences that remove the offender **for the least amount of time** from instruction. Please don't feel like a failure (as I did early in my career).

The critical goal is to **preserve the environment and integrity** you have created and the learning process of the other 99%. If your school has a "restorative center" as does mine, utilize it. The individual assigned to it is receiving a paycheck as are you.

Include your parent(s) in the disciplining of repeat offenders and develop a behavior plan with your parent and administrator. In cases where there are multiple offenders or clicks of offenders **IMMEDIATLEY** have separate restorative conversations with them and inform them that their choices have consequences and that their undesired behaviors are noticed and are of interest to you, the parent, and the administrator.

For those of you that have athlete offenders, remind them that you are a colleague of their coach, and that you and the coach are on the same page when it comes to academics vs. athletics!

Teaching at East Tech has made me realize that not all management practices learned in undergrad are effective. Students will "take you there" if you allow them. They will "push your button" if you expose it; so don't reveal it. Keep your composure, call on Jesus, continue teaching, or simply pause and count to 10. Don't become or make emotional outbursts in the presence of the offender or class. Losing your power is dangerous and you may never get it back 100%.

Dealing with severe behavior is simply a question of what you allow. Just as in chapter 8 what you permit; you promote. In my room, all I have to do is give that look, and students know what time it is. If you are able to get to that point early in your career, any administrator evaluating your classroom management skill set will know that you have established a clear line between what acceptable behaviors are and what is not!

When passing your course matters, grades matter. When grades matter, points matter. When points matter, attendance matters. When attendance matter, you must be in class. If you are in my class, it's because you are abiding by rules and regulations and the established norms and expectations I have created and established. PERIOD!

Is My Leading & Teaching Reaching?

(Part two.)

Chapter 12

Every- is for

Engagement.

The past 11 chapters were dedicated on two major tenants that I believe to be the foundations of operative teaching and the root of what I learned throughout my years from stumbling and being successful:

1. **Taking a daily dose of Personalization, Collaboration and Differentiation; personalize with your kids, collaborate with your colleagues and differentiate instruction to meet all academic needs; *PerCoDiff* and**
2. **The ten strategies to consider when creating a classroom culture of high expectations.**

In the next segment of this resource tool I would like to unpack what I believe is the recipe for effective teaching which ultimately answers a resounding "YES" to the question **"Is my leading & teaching reaching?"** This segment will better prepare you for your walkthrough analysis and what is expected during a walkthrough of your classroom.

For teachers, I pray that you **will reflect** on your teaching pedagogy and teaching practices. For administrators, I anticipate you will train yourself to seek **and identify** student understanding, rigor in lessons, research based engagement strategies, aligned curriculum, instructional decisions your teachers make, walls of student artifacts and the safety of your students and teachers. In the acronym Every Child Is Worthy & Safe, the letter "E" is for *engagement*. Let me unpack what administrators *should* consider when evaluating and noting the engagement of children.

An administrator will instantly notice what students are doing upon entering the room. In only a few seconds the connection between students and the lesson being taught is also noted. The degree to which all students are on task and/or engaged in the lesson is noted as well.

During my short tenure in the Lorain, I read a book by Robert Marzano on engagement strategies that completely changed my life. I attended his lecture in Cleveland in 2005 where he discussed his book and his findings. He justified certain engagement practices as the "most effective" by the number of times he saw them being utilized by "Star" educators.

Mr. Marzano desired to know what where the secrets to great teaching. He spent a few years traveling the country and visiting different schools. During those visits he'd ask the administrator in charge to identify his "standout" teacher(s) and asked for permission to observe them over a time period. As his tour of the country came to a conclusion, Mr. Marzano began **identifying the common thread** that made these educators effective teachers, accomplished teachers, exemplary teachers and thus great educators.

He narrowed his findings to the TOP 9 most effective engagement and teaching practices, the first of which is ***identifying similarities and differences.*** The reason why this strategy ranked #1 of the nine was because it supports what is transpiring in the brain:

- The human brain naturally looks for **connections and relationships** between and among prior and new learning.
- All new learning is internalized and connected to **prior knowledge.** Mr. Marzano noticed that effective teachers:

1. Asked students to compare by identifying similarities and differences among concepts.
2. Helped students classify by grouping things that are alike into categories.
3. Encouraged students to create metaphors by identifying a basic pattern in one item that is reflected in another item.
4. Asked students to create analogies by finding relationships between pairs of concepts. (e.g. "A is to B as C is to D".

Worksheet #1 is a simple "T" chart that reflects identifying similarities and differences. Begin with a concept in mind and allow students to trigger some thinking. Another favorite Silver, Strong, Perini strategy that I enjoy doing is an ***Understanding*** strategy used to compare, contrast, and analyze as students conclude and infer possible causes and effects by choosing two topics to compare. Two overlapping circles help children to draw conclusions by activating prior and existing knowledge about both topics.

Name _____

Concept _____

#1

The second strategy involves ***summarizing and note taking.*** The reason why this strategy ranked #2 of the nine was because it supports what is transpiring in the brain:

- **Relevance and Meaning** are important to the brain. The Brain deletes what is not useful.
- The brain will retain information when there is a **personal connection** to the content.
- The brain will generate possibilities when students are asked to solve "**Real-World Problems**". Mr. Marzano noticed that effective teachers:

1. Taught students the rules to summarizing and using "summary frames" (e.g. narrative, definition, or problem-solution) to highlight important text elements.
2. Gave students teacher-prepared notes and explicitly taught them a variety of note-taking formats (e.g. combination notes, outlines, webs, and summaries).

The third strategy involves ***reinforcing effort and providing recognition.*** The reason Mr. Marzano ranked this strategy #3 is because it supports the brain research that says:

- The brain responds **positively** to challenge and **negatively** to threat. Emotions enhance or negate learning.
- The brain **organizes and stores** information.

- The brain reflects the experiences and conceptual understandings, attitudes, values, skills, and strategies **that students bring** to a text situation. Mr. Marzano noticed that teachers:

1. Explicitly taught students the importance of **effort**.
2. Stopped frequently at students' desks to "**pause, prompt, and praise**".
3. Used stickers and other concrete symbols or recognition **to praise, reward, and acknowledge**.

The fourth strategy involves ***homework and practice.*** The reason Mr. Marzano ranked this strategy #4 is because it supports the brain research that says:

- In order for the brain to store information into <u>long term memory</u> it is necessary to provide opportunities for **guided and independent** practice.
- The brain and learning is <u>situated.</u> Transfer only occurs if there is **deliberate** modeling, scaffolding, and instructional bridging. Mr. Marzano noticed that teachers:

1. Gave students time to practice, review, and apply knowledge to **become efficient** in a skill or process.

2. Established a homework policy that included **consequences** for not completing it and clarified **acceptable** types of parent involvement.
3. Designed homework assignments that **had a clear** purpose, outcome, and focus on specific elements, skills, or processes.

The fifth strategy involves ***nonlinguistic representation.*** The reason Mr. Marzano ranked this strategy #5 is because it supports the brain research that says:

- The brain will recall information with 90% accuracy when the students are given **visual stimuli** like graphic organizers, cause and effect chains, models, movement, pictures or illustrations. Mr. Marzano noticed that teachers:

1. Used **pictures or pictographs** to represent students' new knowledge.
2. Helped students generate **mental pictures** of what they are learning.
3. Used **physical models** (e.g. activities with physical motion) to help them understand what they are learning.

    a) Using the "Cubing in the Content Areas" worksheet is an effective method **to "cube" a new concept or theme.** Also use this cubing chart with the 8th strategy explained in a bit.

b) Using the "Frayer Model" also aids tremendously in **developing** new vocabulary.

c) Using the "What?" chart is another visual stimulus that will help with **recalling information** with accuracy.

Occasionally students require these nonlinguistic representations to enhance the concept or standard you desire for them to grasp. When an art student is struggling with **how three point perspectives** is supposed to look like, it is simpler for them to see an example first. Teaching this concept of "fading" is challenging to communicate. When seen, students are able to generate **mental pictures** of what they are learning.

CUBING in the Content Areas

Content Area _____ Name _____ Date _____

Cubing Concept _____

Describe it:	Consider/ visualize the subject in detail and explain what you see.	
Associate it:	What does it make you think of? Connect it with something.	
Compare it:	To what is it similar? From what is it different? Explain how.	
Apply it:	Tell what you can do with it. How can it be used?	
Analyze it:	Tell how it is made or how it functions. If you don't know, make it up!	
Argue for or against it:	Take a stand. Refer to text and/or prior knowledge to substantiate your stand with reasons.	

Forget 2004, Kuzmich 2009

Frayer Model- Vocabulary Development Tool

Grade Level Indicator: _____

Definition in your own words	Facts/Characteristics
Examples	Non-Examples

Definition in your own words	Facts/Characteristics
Examples	Non-Examples

Definiton in your own words	Facts/Characteristics
Examples	Non-Examples

Definition in your own words	Facts/Characteristics
Examples	Non-Examples

Adapted from: *Differentiated Literacy Strategies*, Gregory & Kuzmich 2005

"What?" Chart

What did I learn?
So, what does this mean to me?
What questions remain?
What will I do with what I learned?

The sixth strategy mostly used by standout teachers is probably the oldest and most used. The strategy of ___cooperative learning___ supports brain research that states:

- The **brain is social** and makes meaning through interaction and **dialogue**.
- Because learning is active the brain constructs meaning through **direct experiences** such as group investigation, peer tutoring, open discussions, and class meetings. Mr. Marzano noticed effective teachers:

1. Placed students in small groups of 3 to 4 students with **well-structured** cooperative learning activities.

2. **Varied** grouping patterns so students aren't always in the same group.
3. **Avoided** ability grouping (e.g. placing students of like ability in the same group) as it impedes the progress of low-ability students.

    a) The "Peer Activities" worksheet is a great reminder to educators on **the type** of partners and small group activities you can do in your lessons.

Paired Reading

Partners decide on roles of **teller** and **listener**.

Both partners perform silent reading, mentally paraphrasing.

(Books closed) **Teller** recalls as much as possible while listener listens.

(Books closed) **Listener** then adds more information if possible.

Both open books, scan for missed detail, discuss, swap roles.

Inside-Outside Circle

Inside and outside circles of students face each other.

Within each pair of facing students, students quiz each other with questions they have written.

Outside circle moves to create new pairs.

Repeat.

Reciprocal Teaching

Predict – one student predicts what he thinks the passage will be about.
Question – one student **in the group of four** generates some questions that he/she thinks will be answered in the passage
Summarize – after all four have read the passage, one student will identify key points & develop short summary.
Clarify – Student will paraphrase, restate, deepen understanding of passage.
Each group-of-four reports out.

Paired Writing

Two writers engage in the process together. They discuss ideas and vocabulary. The shared task builds synergy and confidence.

Peer Activities

Partners
Small Groups

Flexible Grouping

Organize groups (of 3 or 4 students) by learning style, need, or content, but not by "life sentence."

Information Circle

Students in the circle take on specific roles. For example:
- Discussion Manager
- Vocabulary Manager
- Illustrator
- Connector/Reflector
- Clarifier
- Summarizer

Book Ends

Pairs of students discuss and make predictions before an activity, then meet after the activity to review and compare reactions

Think-Pair-Share

Teacher poses questions or ideas about the selected reading.

Students think about the question or idea on their own, then turn to a partner and discuss their thoughts about the question or idea.

Students can share their partner's or their own understanding (orally or in writing).

*"The brain is social
and desires opportunities to process and make meaning
through interaction and dialogue."*

Adapted from *Differentiated Learning Strategies*, Gregory & Kuzmich, 2005; *Max Teaching*, Forget, 2004

The 7th ranked strategy of ***setting objectives and providing feedback*** supports the findings of research which says the brain:

- The brain likes purpose and relaxed alertness. **High challenge and low threat** are optimal and necessary for learners.

- **Learning is at its best when** students understand it purpose, can articulate personal goals, and monitor their own progress. Mr. Marzano noted that effective teachers:

1. Helped students set learning goals that are **specific and personal** (e.g. I want to know why Ice age animals were so big.)

2. Provided students with feedback that's corrective in nature by **explaining why** an answer is incorrect.

3. Used criterion-referenced (rubrics) feedback to inform students of their progress toward **learning specific knowledge**, not simply how they compare with peers.

4. When it came to high school graduation assessment requirements, students know where they stand, what their "story" is, and the score they required for being proficient.

Concept _____

K What I Know	
I What Interests Me	
C What Choices I Have	

a) The "KIC" chart above is simple and easy to use in assessing **what you think students should know**. I use this when giving pre-tests or when ascertaining prior knowledge.

The 8th ranked strategy mostly used by teachers involve ***generating and testing hypothesis.*** The brain research supports this strategy because the brain:

- Is curious and seeks meaning and clarity **though patterns**.

- Requires support in drawing conclusions. **Asking students "What if?"** while they are conducting investigations will ensure analytical thinking for text and information sources. Mr. Marzano noticed that effective teachers:

1. Encouraged students to generate hypothesis by using both **deductive** (predicting from a general rule) and **inductive** (developing rules from observations) reasoning.

2. Asked students to **clearly explain** their hypothesis and conclusions.

3. Used a variety of **structured tasks** (e.g. systems analysis, problem solving, historical investigation, invention) to develop students' higher level thinking skills.

   a) I use the "Analytical Thinking for Text or Information Sources" worksheet when I assign group projects or individual project based learning assignments. This sheet can also be used as a basis for establishing criteria and/or grading purposes.

ANALYTIC THINKING
for
TEXT or INFORMATION SOURCES

1. What is the purpose of this material?

2. What is a key question that is addressed or needs to be addressed?

3. What is the most important information?

4. What are the main inferences that can be made?

5. What are the key ideas or concepts?

6. What are the assumptions the author(s) made in this information, issue, or source?

7. What are the implications of this information?

8. What is the main point of view that is presented?

8

The average percentile points gained on Student Achievement Tests suggest that there is a:
1. 45% increase with strategy 1.
2. 34% increase with strategy 2.
3. 29% increase with strategy 3.
4. 28% increase with strategy 4.
5. 27% increase with strategies 5 & 6.
6. 23% increase with strategies 7 & 8 and
7. 22% increase with this 9th strategy:

The last strategy is noted as the 9th mostly used strategy involving ***cues, questions, and advance organizers***. The brain research totally agrees with these because:

- The brain appreciates wholes and parts. It **needs mental constructs** on which to hook new learning.
- The brain **anticipates** new information when a student activates prior knowledge first!
- The brain is most productive to students' thinking **when they are asked open-ended questions.** Mr. Marzano noticed that effective teachers:

1. Began a unit or new lessons **using cues** (e.g. hints about what students are going to learn) to help students retrieve, use, and organize what they **already know** about a topic.

2. **Waited briefly** before accepting responses from students to increase the depth of their answers.

3. Used advanced organizers (e.g. stories, videos, skimming reading passages, graphics) to prepare students to **learn new content** especially when the content is poorly organized (e.g. field trip).

    a) Using the "Anticipation Guide" worksheet was helpful in class or group discussions as well as **provoking** thought organization.

Anticipation Guide

Title of Lesson: _____

Before reading the assigned text selection:
In the space to the left of each statement, place a check mark (✓) if you agree or think the statement is true. Discuss your interpretations with your partner or small group members.

During or after reading:
Add new check marks or cross through those about which you have changed your mind.

Keep in mind that this is not like the traditional "worksheet." You may have to put on your thinking caps and "read between the lines." Use the space under each statement to note the page(s), and paragraph(s) where you are finding information to support your thinking. Discuss your logic with your group before giving your final answer.

_____ 1. _____

_____ 2. _____

_____ 3. _____

_____ 4. _____

_____ 5. _____

_____ 6. _____

Teachers, when you consider if your engagement is on point, or whether your engagement of students will be considered effectual during your walkthrough, strongly consider **these details** along with the implementation of one of the nine strategies aforementioned:

- ✓ Greet your class at the door.
- ✓ Give precise directions.
- ✓ Narrate who is following your direction so those that aren't have a chance to get going.
- ✓ Provide a bell ringer on yesterday's lesson.
- ✓ Plan to re-teach if your Bell ringer data is deficient.
- ✓ Look enthused as it is an important factor in student motivation, which is closely linked to achievement.
- ✓ Articulate the standard or the lesson's objective.
- ✓ Present the "Big Picture".
- ✓ Activate prior knowledge.
- ✓ Have students make predictions.
- ✓ Have students read and think aloud.
- ✓ Model student connection to self, text, or world.
- ✓ Precisely explain what will be used as the assessment.
- ✓ Provide support (scaffolding) when needed.
- ✓ Utilize classroom centers; reading, writing, research, and discussion areas.
- ✓ Explain what will be the evidence of mastery.
- ✓ Plan instruction accordingly.
- ✓ Encourage student questioning-the shortest route to teaching content.
- ✓ Engage in a quick review.
- ✓ Provide an exit ticket on the day's work learned.

Here are some **"Don'ts of Engagement"** that should be avoided at all costs. Why? Because they will provide the exact opposite of what is the 100% engagement goal. These are the biggest learning challenges that I have learned and identified (and believe me I have been there, done that) from years of teaching:

- ❖ Rote & Routine Learning: change it up. Don't get caught in the same old, same old.
- ❖ Drill: lacks interest and can hurt learning.
- ❖ Memorization: after the test, the information is lost and forgotten.
- ❖ Stress: they will simply shut down!
- ❖ Conflict: they will win; you will lose your power.
- ❖ Apathy: they know when all you're doing is collecting a paycheck.
- ❖ Independent Working: they require precise directions and models of acceptable work.
- ❖ Uninteresting Information: Make it relevant!
- ❖ Repetition: You will lose their interest!

No matter which way you attempt to cover these or decorate these "Don'ts" they **will** cause you heartache and chaos. As an administrator and observer of "bad" teaching, these were the practices being used in classrooms with struggling teachers. I would inspire you to avoid them at ALL COSTS!

Here are some final tips and thoughts when considering engagement **from and evaluator's point** of view:

➢ **The probability of engagement increases when students see what they are doing as meaningful and relevant to their lives and directly related to district and the state assessment. Does teacher invent work that engages all students?**

➢ **Lessons should be arranged in clear and accessible ways.**

➢ **Lessons should be focused on a product or performance of significance to students.**

➢ **Lessons should assign tasks without fear of embarrassment, punishments, or other implications.**

➢ **Lessons should assign work that encourages and supports opportunities for students to work with others.**

➢ **Work should be visible and important to others.**

➢ **Lessons should expose students to new and different ways of doing things.**

➢ **Lessons should be creative that produce new forms of work and new products.**

Remember, the goal of engagement is that 100% of the students in the room are involved and on task with the work at hand. Be careful with enabling teachers who allow student's issues to overcome the importance of their education. If relationships are sacred (and they should be), students experiencing hardships and drama will release their burdens out of the respect and love they have for their teachers and the standard of educational importance they have set in that classroom.

Chapter 13

Child- is for

Curriculum.

In the acronym Every Child Is Worthy & Safe, the letter "C" is for *curriculum.* During a walkthrough administrators note the learning objective being taught. It is the goal of the walkthrough to determine if mother curriculum and her "quadruplets" are in the lesson being presented. Curriculum is comprised of four components that I refer to as the children of mother curriculum. These components are easy to remember because they all compliment the letter "c". Content, cognitive, context, and congruency should be noted upon entering the room.

The first of the quadruplets is **content.** Content is the skill, knowledge, process, and concept to be learned. What is being delivered? If you are in a data driven district as am I, you will become good friends with the Common Core Quick Flip Reference Booklet, your district scope and sequence guide, your state's standard-benchmark-grade level indicator manual, or your content's suggested pacing guide.

I always post the daily objective on my smart board for the students **to see when walking into my room.** They are trained to read it and sometimes record it in their interactive notebook upon entering the classroom.

I encouraged this behavior because I aim to be prepared for an administrator (or visitor) to sneak in and ask one of my kids, "What are you learning today?"

It is absolutely OK for a student to read the objective off the smart board (poster or wall). This will satisfy any ambiguity that an administrator has if they are unclear about what is being taught. This protocol should be explained to students in **your first five days** of the year. Always be prepared for an unannounced walkthrough of your room.

For EVERY assignment, project, or test, you should publish **in advance** the expectations for "proficient" work. The best way to do this is to create a rubric. It will save you from having to explain why students earned the grade they see on their electronic grade book. If your rubrics are clear and precise, students should spontaneously be able to explain what "proficient" work is for each assignment/assessment and understand why they earned the grade that appears.

If you are a follower of Grant Wiggins and Jay McTighe like me you will try the **Backward Design** process which is broken down into three stages:

1. Identify **Desired results**
2. Determine **Acceptable Evidence** and
3. Plan **Learning Experiences & Instruction**

For me and my students, the backward design enables me, as a reflective practitioner, to answer three critical questions about the day and the lesson:

1. **What** are my babies going to do today in class?
2. **Why** are they going to do what I've asked them to do?
3. **How** will I know if my students have been successful in doing "it" whatever "it" is?   (exit ticket)

Adding the words "Students can…" to the **standard** being taught is an instant objective for your written lesson plan. **Make standards visible** in the classroom and express them in language that students and administrators understand (as well as parents.)

In some classrooms I observed, effective teachers will have students do an "I can" statement before the class ends; another great teaching idea! Remember that your **benchmarks** are the concepts to be tested on. I recommend you teach these concepts deeply (less is more**).** It is far more effective to be a mile long and a mile deep than three miles long and one inch deep!

The **indicators** (the skills students pick up when teachers teach benchmarks), should be utilized to gauge whether or not your benchmarks are being mastered on tests and other assessment tools. **Just because something was "covered" does not mean that students learned it. If they "forgot it" they never learned it!**

The second child of mother curriculum is **context.** What are your thoughts on context?

Does your philosophy of context match that of your principal and/or district? <u>Context</u> is the condition under which students **will demonstrate** that learning has happened. Reflect on your modes of response, materials, and the information that is provided for students orally or written. In other words ask yourself in what framework do I deliver my objectives?

- Examine the tests and worksheets (ARTIFACTS) you are giving your students.

ASK YOURSELF…..

- **Is the student evaluation tied to a Common Core Standard, State Standard, and District Standard?**
- **Do I provide feedback to my students and parents about the quality of the student work when compared to the standard?**
- **Do I look at my artifacts (my handouts or worksheets) to make certain they are not all remembering and understanding? Do my artifacts reflect variety levels of Bloom's?**
- **Do my tests look like State and District Assessments? Instead of giving my babies the traditional bubble or multiple choice tests, I began looking at some other assessment styles that would offer my kids "other" ways to show off what they really knew. Here are some:**

1)   EXTENDED RESPONSES
2)   ANECDOTAL RECORDS
3)   PROBLEM/SOLUTION
4)   SHORT RESPONSES
5)   EXPERIMENT RECORDING

6) RESEARCH PROJECTS
7) INTERACTIVE JOURNALS
8) DEBATES
9) ORAL PRESENTATIONS
10) PORTFOLIOS
11) GRADE LEVEL INDICATOR QUIZZES
12) SUMMARIES
13) CONTRAST/COMPARE
14) CAUSE/EFFECT

If your kids are sick and tired of the normal 30 to 40 questions of multiple choice tests like mine, I would ask of you, beg you, to consider 1 through 14 above. After teaching the unit of "La Familia", I began thinking of other ways to assess my students. Even though it was uncomfortable for me to think out of the box, I gave my first year's a chance to present their test (#9).

I laid the template for presenting family members to the class, provided a rubric for proficient work, modeled what my final desired work should sound and look like, and asked them to bring in (at minimum) pictures of 6 family members they could introduce, tell us their names, their relationship, two adjectives to describe each, and what they liked and disliked, (all standards that were taught in the quarter). Like the trip to "El Rincón Criollo", this lesson turned out to be one of the most enjoyable lessons of the year.

I had the opportunity to walk-through a Spanish lesson of one of my colleagues when she allowed the students to do something similar when finishing the unit on "Ir de compras", going shopping. The students converted the classroom into a store.

They were allowed to move about the room purchasing items, (with monopoly money) using the vocabulary, phrases and grammar they had learned all quarter. It was "controlled chaos" at its best, enjoyable to observe, and for the students was an enjoyable assessment. Señora Olivera had provided a rubric with clear criteria as to what was acceptable and what the expectations were. She **facilitated** the assessment as she walked about with half sheet of what appeared to be each student's name and continued to give them marks for their efforts or lack thereof. ¡Bravo!

The third quadruplet of mother curriculum is cognitive. **<u>Cognitive</u>** is the thinking level at which the instruction is being delivered. Teachers should constantly ask themselves, do I teach at the Remember (knowledge) and Understand (comprehension) levels too much? What about the higher levels of the revised Bloom's Taxonomy such as:

- **Create (evaluation),**
- **Evaluate (synthesis),**
- **Analyze (analysis),**
- **Apply (application).**

How can I tap into these areas of the brain without causing my babies stress or fear? This, over the past 20 years has been the most challenging and frustrating. Why; because my students are not used to triggering high levels of critical thinking, or problem solving.

Before the school year began I went to a printing store and had life size posters made of the revised Bloom's Taxonomy and the "Quadrant D" worksheet of

Barbara Fowler's *Critical Thinking Across Curriculum (1996).* The goal was to have these visible in EVERY room of the building so that ALL stakeholders could see and read them everywhere they turned.

I understood that in order to get my learning communities to buy into this idea of rigorous thinking, I had to convince my teachers to strive to include questions that require *rigorous thinking* when creating, selecting, and modifying assessments **and** learning activities.

Like students, I knew that if my teachers saw visuals, they would make an effort (I prayed) to begin tapping into these high level (but dormant) cognitive domains. Adding the "power verbs" and sample "open ended questions" to these posters was THE BEST idea ever. Administrators should consider using these, if achieving and firing of high levels of rigorous thinking, is a building goal for students.

The ultimate goal of teaching and learning is to get your students to Quadrant D where they take the information they have learned to answer a question or solve a problem thus unpacking critical thinking and problem solving!

During walkthroughs of your room your administrator should note if the "thinking" of the lessons are always being conducted at the *remembering, understanding, and applying levels* or do the lesson(s) reach Quadrant D and ask:

- Can students distinguish between parts? Are you asking your students to compare, contrast, criticize, question, differentiate, discriminate, distinguish, examine, experiment, synthesize and test?…ANALYZE.
- Can students justify a stand or decision? Do you ask your students to appraise, argue, defend, judge, select, support, value or evaluate? ....EVALUATE.
- Can your students create a new product or point of view? Do your babies know how to assemble, construct, create, design, develop, formulate or write? …..CREATE.

If you have set your room barometer at elevated levels of thinking, these three highest levels of Bloom's will begin to manifest daily. Your administrator will begin to **notice and observe** the positive implications on district and state tests as you march across the passage of poor performance into continuous improvement.

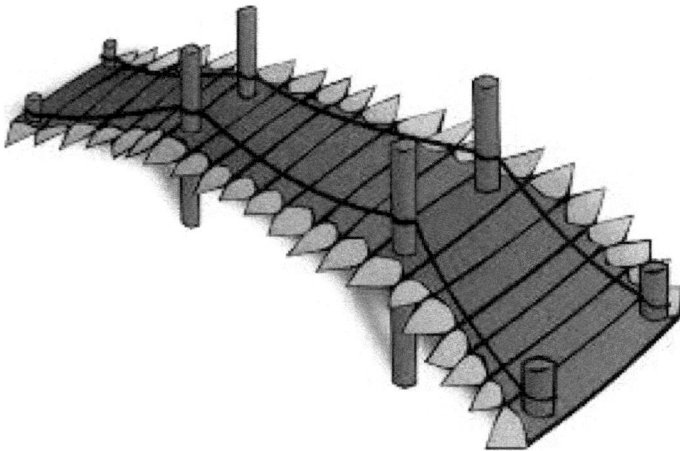

BLOOM'S REVISED TAXONOMY

Creating
Generating new ideas, products, or ways of viewing
things
Designing, constructing, planning, producing, inventing.

Evaluating
Justifying a decision or course of action
Checking, hypothesizing, critiquing, experimenting, judging

Analysing
Breaking information into parts to explore understandings
and relationships
Comparing, organizing, deconstructing, interrogating,
finding

Applying
Using information in another familiar situation
Implementing, carrying out, using, executing

Understanding
Explaining ideas or concepts
Interpreting, summarizing, paraphrasing, classifying,
explaining

Remembering
Recalling information
Recognizing, listing, describing, retrieving, naming, finding

Standard:			The Task
Quadrant D	Create	Can the student create a new product or point of view? *assemble, construct, create, design, develop, formulate, write*	
	Evaluate	Can the student justify a stand or decision? *appraise, argue, defend, judge, select, support, value, evaluate*	
	Analyze	Can the student distinguish between the different parts? *compare, contrast, criticize, question, differentiate, discriminate, distinguish, examine, experiment, synthesize, test*	
	Apply	Can the student use the information in a new way? *choose, demonstrate, dramatize, employ, illustrate, interpret, operate, schedule, sketch, solve, use, write*	
	Understand	Can the student explain ideas or concepts? *classify, describe, discuss, explain, identify, locate, recognize, report, select, translate, paraphrase*	
	Remember	Can the student recall or remember the information? *define, duplicate, list, memorize, recall, repeat, reproduce, state*	

The last baby of curriculum is congruency. **Congruency** is noted with the Xerox copies, handouts, and worksheets (artifacts) that are given to students. At some point in the first quarter your classroom will hopefully have some artifacts of work hanging on a designated bulletin board. Your administrator should begin giving you feedback on the congruency of those artifacts. Before he does, I would advise you to ask yourself are they aligned and congruent to the objective being taught? Or are they "busy work"? How about the movies I show or the field trips we take? Do I make a connection in everything we do with the standard at hand?

So far we have discussed two major components of a walkthrough from two points of view; what an administrator is seeking or noting upon entering your room and whether or not the teaching you are doing is reaching your students. The desired goal is 100% engagement and to have all four "quadruplets" in the play pen (your classroom).

To sum up mother curriculum consider:

- **Making Mother Curriculum exciting, relevant and personal.**
- **Nurturing her 4 "C's": Content, Context, Cognitive, and Congruent levels must match what will be expected on state and districts assessments.**
- **Doctrine of "no surprises" – teach what is being tested, teach it deeply, teach it to the level it will be tested, test it, check learning, re-teach as needed.**

- Let students know objectives and expectations ahead of time.
- Taught, tested, and written curriculum should be in deep alignment and you should constantly be reflecting and asking yourself these essential questions:

  i. Am I teaching the right stuff?
  ii. Am I teaching it in the right context and at the right level of Bloom's?
  iii. Are my students learning it?
  iv. What am I doing when they are not learning?
  v. The Standards; are they up, posted, displayed, seen, and recent?

Always strive to make the curriculum you are supposed to teach **connect to what is relevant** in the lives of those you are teaching the curriculum to.

Chapter 14

Is- is for

Instruction.

In the acronym Every Child <u>Is</u> Worthy & Safe, the letter "I" is for *instruction*. The instructional strategies or strategy being used to teach the lesson are noticed by your administrator. The <u>decisions</u> that you, the teacher, has made regarding your lesson and how that <u>decision</u> has informed the teaching practices being employed are also considered during a walk through.

Earlier in the book I referenced Robert Marzano and his wonderful book *"Classroom Instruction That Works…."*and the 9 strategies that he proves enhances and improves student achievement. As an educator I found these strategies to be things that I have done for years that were now given a clever name and determined to be "effective and optimal" for teaching and learning. They do work! They are the preeminent nine strategies in teaching at all levels of education. For this reason the administrator conducting your walkthrough who is considered the instructional leader in your building, should be capable in identifying when you are using these researched based strategies. Unfortunately, most administrators won't be adept to recognizing the official strategy name. So it's up to you to pinpoint it and bring it to light during your evaluation.

Make certain to annotate that some teacher decisions you have made *are* research based and effective in the learning of your students. In addition to the Marzano 9 I have also applied these other instructional methodologies that for me have proven to aid tremendously in the teaching and learning process:

1. **Differentiate instruction by creating centers.**
2. **Implement the gradual release model of teaching discussed in chapter 3.**
3. **Limit direct teaching in large blocks of time.**
4. **Re-group according to mastery and non-mastery (Mainly by tracking bell ringers and exit tickets).**
5. **Vary procedure for establishing small groups through interest, ability and re-teaching.**
6. **Plan some days for individual work and monitoring.**
7. **Plan some days (mainly Friday's) for assessment.**
8. **Plan to re-teach concepts that were not mastered.**
9. **Plan for tiered assignments when they are necessary.**
10. **Introduce and display the objective for the lesson.**

Always ask yourself, "When can I use.....?:

    a. Read aloud
    b. Think aloud
    c. Shared and Guided reading
    d. KWL charts
    e. Vocabulary Instruction

f. Graphic Organizers
g. Structured note taking
h. Reciprocal teaching
i. Peer teaching
j. Writing-To-Learn like:
    i. Daily Journals
    ii. Listen-Stop-Write
    iii. Discuss-Explain-Write
    iv. Question-All-Write

A good practice to get into is to always look for feedback from your students to determine their attention levels, relevancy to their lives, and when necessary, make adjustments that you feel **will best fit** who you are as an educator. Again, these practices aren't meant to be followed as a recipe. They are meant to trigger ideas on how you can tweak them to better suit your style of teaching based on your personality, experiences, and the students your serve.

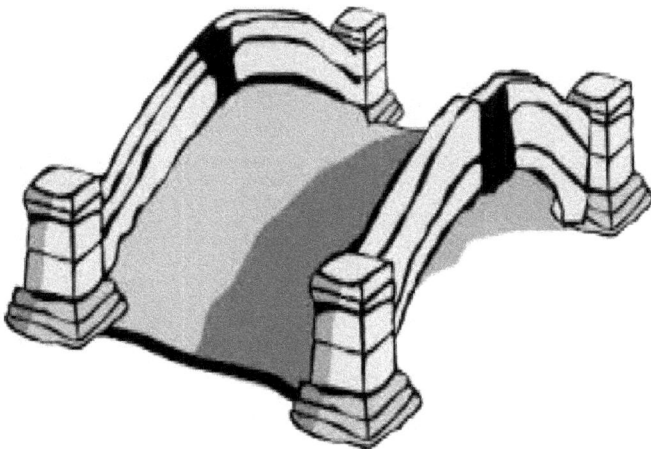

Read Alouds

Please plan to read to your students everyday for at least five minutes in your subject area.

Students may listen as the teacher reads aloud or students may read along.

You may choose to select other materials that: build students' background knowledge, provide them with interesting vocabulary, and ensure that they are hearing fluent reading.

Reciprocal Teaching

Students work in groups of four reading a passage together.

They follow a protocol for predicting, questioning, clarifying, and summarizing.

These skills have been modeled over a series of lessons until students are comfortable assuming the assigned roles.

KWL Charts

After the grade level indicator for the lesson has been introduced, simply ask the question—
"What do you _know_ about the topic?"

Discussion follows! (Answers can be recorded on chart paper).

"What do you still _want_ to know about the topic?"

After the lesson, students answer the third question, "What did you _learn_ about the topic?"

Written or oral responses are received.

Structured Notetaking

Students draw a vertical line about two inches from the left side of the paper.

They log main ideas and key words to the left and details to the right of the line,

and write a brief summary of the lesson at the bottom of the page.

Vocabulary Instruction

Utilization of vocabulary journals—
Ask students to fill out four columns in their vocabulary journal.

Column 1: list words
Column 2: write common definition
Column 3: write subject definition
Column 4: students identify where they found the definitions

Graphic Organizers

Graphic organizers provide students with visual information that:
compliments the class discussion or text and highlights relationships between concepts being studied.

Examples of graphic organizers include: prediction charts, word maps, t squares, webs, story maps, category organizers, main idea charts, sequence charts.

Writing-to-Learn

Teachers use this writing-to-learn strategy at the beginning, middle, and end of class to help students inquire, clarify, or reflect on the content.

Writing helps students think about the content and reflect on their knowledge of the content.

Students share these thoughts with the class and teacher.

Listen-Stop-Write

Listen-Stop-Write involves breaking the lecture into three-minute segments interspersed with two-minute writing periods.

When modeled and developed, this technique will help students focus on their listening and notetaking.

If your district is big on reading make a cavalier attempt to incorporate shelter reading in all that you do. If you are an administrator, you should inspire reading in **ALL your rooms** regardless of the content being taught. As a learner and educator of second language acquisition, I always honored teachers who embraced the <u>Sheltered Instructional Operational Protocol</u> which embeds and uses reading strategies to improve student's achievement and scores on assessments. In my years of walking through ELA and Dual Language rooms, here are various reading strategies that I noted worked effectively to help children acquire both targeted languages.

My teachers made sure to:

1. **Make students aware of textbook organization (description, sequence, contrast and comparison, cause and effect, problem and solution).**
2. **Present the big picture.**
3. **Make connections for students as to how lesson relates to the big picture.**
4. **Encourage student questions.**
5. **Introduce vocabulary and break words into syllables, and write definitions in an interactive notebook.**
6. **Read silently for specific purpose.**
7. **Visualize while reading to students**
8. **Make inferences.**
9. **Direct student attention to most important ideas in text.**
10. **Stop at end of each page and ask for summaries.**
11. **Think aloud while reading aloud to the class.**

12. Check often for understanding.
13. Provide read aloud opportunities linked to specific purpose. Never do "round robins" and always allow students to verbalize thoughts while reading orally.
14. Encourage students to discuss, explain, and write alone or with partners.
15. Employ before, during, and after-reading strategies (predicting, monitoring, inferring, drawing conclusions, and summarizing).
16. Provide a system for students to document the reading they do in interactive notebook or on exit ticket.

These **sixteen reading strategies** have no impressive names but they are protocols that aid in the development of reading. I would embolden you to use and document their usage so that they speak to the onstage instruction you are evaluated on. It never harms to provide administrators with the evidence you do in your room, work that they may not have noted during a walkthrough of your lesson.

Reflect on these thoughts when you consider the choices you make in the instruction of your students:

- **Realize that YOU are the only variable YOU have any control over.**
    - **I cannot control who my students are or what their baggage is.**
    - **I cannot control what parents do or DON'T DO at home.**
    - **I cannot control the outcomes – the state does.**

- Learning Strategies should be valid, research-based strategies.
- Student work (and homework) must align to desired outcomes.
- Strive to make lessons relevant to students.
- Convince students that success is related to effort.
- Build in scaffolds to reach all students
    - Build safety nets for students (students that need help)
    - Time is variable – goal is for ALL students to achieve (reduce too much "free time") TIME ON TASK! YOU ONLY HAVE 180 DAYS!
    - Change belief system – failure is not an option!
- Include classes of interaction between you and students.
- Continue on-going formative assessments. Use formative assessments to drive instruction- ALWAYS.
- Allow students to revisit, revise, and resubmit substandard work {the 3 rs). Give them rubrics to follow.

REFLECTREFLECTREFLECTREFLECTREFLECTREFLECT

- Indispensable questions:
    - Are my students reaching the objectives?
    - If not, how can that objective be taught again?
    - How is formative and summative data being used to change instruction?
    - When students do not demonstrate success, can I do something differently?
    - When class is over ask yourself if lesson affected student achievement?
    - Did my lesson work? If yes, do more of it. If not, stop doing it!

Chapter 15

Worthy- is for

Walls of Work.

In the acronym Every Child Is <u>W</u>orthy & Safe, the letter "W" is for *walls of work*. An administrator will quickly notice the artifacts that are posted to the walls in your classroom. The walls often speak to the <u>unspoken, extended, and human</u> nature of curriculum in the classroom. Student or teacher work, lesson plans, lesson extensions and invitations to new learning are examples of salient information that can be gleaned by noting what's on the walls.

When you are self-reflecting about the work you are posting on the walls think about these things:

- Am I using my standards booklet(s); my state content standards guide, and or my district scope and sequence to make certain that my worksheets are deeply aligned?
- Am I analyzing some of my worksheets with Bloom's to make certain they are tapping into Quadrant D thinking and congruent to the standard at hand?
- During grade level meetings or departmental meetings one of the things I required my teams to do was to select an artifact they have passed out in class to children and conduct an "**ARTIFACT-ASSESSMENT ANAYLYSIS PROTOCOL**":

1. First, teachers were asked to describe the sample of work, its grade level, content area, and the grade level indicator or standard it focused on.
2. Secondly, they were to highlight the highest level of Bloom's that was reflective on the worksheet.
3. Third, list some recommendations for improving the worksheet.
4. Next, identify what specific skills the students required in order to complete this assignment.
5. Finally, discuss and recommend what strategies might be most effective for this lesson.

Grade level teams should do this activity to determine whether the worksheets and tests they are providing children to do, are meeting and exceeding the standard they are teaching. **The examination of student work AND assessments** are treasured in so many ways. The implications this protocol creates for driving instruction are the decisive goals in teaching. If students are bombing question #6 which had to do with "text inference" (as an example) then it ought to inform the educator that this standard requires re-teaching and more explicit strategies geared toward improving and thus mastering that standard.

The dire implications of **examining student work and assessments** are to understand that:

✓ Student work is the most **valuable data** we have.
✓ All other reforms, such as small schools, cooperative learning, extended classroom, and many other researched "best practices" **will only scratch** the surface if work is not aligned and rigorous.

- ✓ The point of **greatest impact** on student learning is the assignment, the exercise, the task, the work that teachers routinely give students.
- ✓ The **feedback** which students and parents **receive** when the aligned work is returned is equally significant.
- ✓ The shortest route to **moving up** the academic ladder is through curriculum alignment.
- ✓ We can only **move from topological alignment to deep alignment** through the examination of student work.
- ✓ It is not what we do, but the **consistency** with which we do it!
- ✓ We need **more information** than what we receive from test scores.
- ✓ Collaborative (remember PerCoDiff) examination of student work will give information about **real knowledge** and skill that kids have or lack.
- ✓ Educators can share work and assessments and **analyze where the areas** of needed improvement are.
- ✓ A process for examining student work and assessments will make the teacher and administrator **more accountable**!
- ✓ Student work and assessment **disaggregation** does not lie!
- ✓ What gets **monitored** by the administrator and teacher team gets done!

The teachers at Tech call this process TBTT, teacher based teaching time, dedicated on every Wednesday to facilitate this protocol. The implications have proven to be most effective in the meeting and exceeding of standards and thus a significant influx in state, district, and classroom assessments.

Chapter 16

Safe- is for

Safety & Security.

In the acronym Every Child Is Worthy & <u>S</u>afe, the letter "S" is for *safety & security* of children. Any safety and/or security issues that may compromise the well-being of students will always be noted during a walkthrough of your lesson. This includes the order of the room, how things are stored, and if the room might cause <u>*academic anxiety*</u> due to disarray or lack of organization on the part of the teacher and students themselves.

Because of East Tech's geographical location in the city of Cleveland, it has the reputation for being one of the most volatile schools, not by what occurs within its walls, but what transpires in the community that surrounds it. With that thought, the security of students and their safety is always at the forefront of the awareness of the adults charged with protecting them and making certain that they experience an environment that is stress less and fear less. Safety is an essential need when teaching in urban America both physical safety and psychological safety.

If you remember the characters in the movies "Finding Forrester" and "The Blind Side", the one essential requisite of both fellows was the feeling of safety and security that both yearned for if not from a biological parent, from a teacher. Our children continuously seek to have a trusting relationship (with adults they have confidence in and can rely on) to be there through hardships. They also pursue a neutral place, an environment that is safe and harmonious to interchange and gain knowledge in.

Throughout my years of teaching in this city I learned to improve a **"Tool"** that helped me to gage and reflect on some of my <u>teacher actions.</u> I began asking myself if I in fact, built safe trusting and harmonious relationships with my students; **a<u>ll</u>**, some, or most? So I commenced to ask my babies what it was about their favorite teachers they revered. These are what individual students expressed to me throughout my years about "**my favorite teacher**...."

- **Cares about me individually**
- **Attends to my interests**
- **Easy to talk to**
- **Makes me feel OK about myself**
- **Knows how I learn best**
- **Knows me personally**
- **Knows what I am feeling**
- **Listens to me when I have a problem**
- **Doesn't hold a grudge**
- **Is Fair**
- **Gives me a second chance**
- **Shows no favoritism**
- **Doesn't humiliate me in front of others**
- **Encourages me to try**
- **Explains work carefully**
- **Helps me learn**
- **Makes sure I have learned**
- **Helps me learn from mistakes**

- Makes work interesting
- Is passionate about teaching
- Explains policies and why they are being enforced
- Is relaxed and can laugh at own mistakes
- Likes me even if I mess up
- Talks to me not at me
- Knows that school may not be MY PRIORITY right now

These 25 responses were at the topmost of hundreds and hundreds of private notes that I collected at the end of each year from students I taught, coached, advised, and mentored. For this main reason is why I decided to write this book, this resource tool. I thought and still believe that most kids don't possess the moral courage to just come out and say these things to the educators they face on a daily base. So I decided to give them a voice.

I believe if you reflect on these while you are blessed to have children to teach, you will become and evolve into a **life changer of kids**. It's conjecture at best, but I think maybe those teachers that Robert Marzano visited and observed would all agree these are the things students say about them. Conversely, during my decade in administration, I would venture to say that most of the gurus I evaluated and identified as "Accomplished" I could attribute these characteristics to them. When Christy Nickerson, mentioned in my dedication, placed a roll of Life-Savers with a *hand written* note that read, "This is what you are to me and your students", I grasped that **I was more** than a teacher of young people and an employee of a school.

Chapter 17

Okay,

now what ?

These last sixteen chapters have focused on answering the initial question, "What does my administrator observe, what is being noted, and what are the expectations during a walkthrough of my classroom?"

In an attempt to prepare you for conducting evaluation of teachers (from an administrative lens) and what practices should be employed and implemented (from a teacher's lens); these strategies and best practices have been extrapolated from a diverse pool of proven researchers, educators, guides, texts, attended conferences, keynote speakers, standout teachers, "Not Yet" teachers, and humbly by me and my own trials and errors, (which have shaped me into the educator that I am today).

So now what? What should materialize after all of the preparation, implementation, and walkthroughs have occurred during the week, quarter and year? Unfortunately, because of all the palaver that happens in administration, more than 50% of administrators do not follow through with the data they have composed form their walkthroughs of respective rooms. There is nothing more vexing and unacceptable to a teacher after being visited and **not receive** feedback of any sort.

Equally disappointing is an administrator not being able to give responses especially if it was a pleasurable walkthrough or if there was a red flag that required some abrupt feedback!

Remember that walkthroughs are supposed to be non-threatening, and quiet, administrators are duty-bound to not conduct walkthroughs with paper and pencil in hand. They should train themselves to recall the components of Every Child Is Worthy & Safe first, and discipline themselves to take notes **outside of the classroom.** Administrators shouldn't make a grand entrance or greet children or the teacher. Just a quick quiet entrance and up to 2 or 3 minutes of noticing and perceiving should suffice.

It took me a year or so to get accustomed to **leaving the room** after the walkthrough and script my notes on an index card (which was in my pocket) **just outside the room** so that I wouldn't disremember what I noted and observed. Jotting down my notes **away from the teachers** kept the stigma of evaluation at bay and made for a more comfortable relationship when entering rooms. The students were used to seeing me, the teacher didn't get all nervous, and the lesson continued as if I wasn't even in the room. At this point (after five or six walkthroughs of a classroom), I had sufficient evidence or data compiled to move into the next phase of the actual walkthrough practice which is **giving feedback.**

I used my pocket index cards to inform my evaluations. Ultimately I yearned to be reasonable in my evaluations and to genuinely inform teachers of the virtuous things I noticed as well as the things I sensed required care or reflection. These are the reasons why walkthroughs cards are so crucial; because they:

- **Identify professional growth topics.**
- **Trigger non-threatening conversations.**
- **Trigger reflective professional thought.**
- **Allow significant growth for teachers/principal partnership.**
- **Allow significant growth for teacher/teacher partnerships and collaboration.**

Walkthrough feedback was never conducted in my office behind a closed door with me at my desk and the teacher in the chair in front of my desk (unless totally necessary). Discussions were sparked in passing, in a morning greeting or afternoon greeting, in the teacher's lounge, or simply by stopping by during a planning period. In Carolyn Downey's book, *"The Three-Minute Classroom Walk-Through"*, she categorized her discussions into three types of statements and three types of questions that ought to be asked in feedback.

The first of the statements administrators can provide is a **Direct Statement.** This kind of statement is usually obliged when administrators observe or note red flags they feel need **immediate** attention and clarification. "Ms. Smith I notice that every time I do a walkthrough Raquan always has his head down in the back of the room". To follow this direct statement an administrator should follow up with a **Direct Question:** "Is there a way I can assist you with him to ensure he is provided the same education as the rest of your scholars?"

The second of the statements you can provide is a **Reflective Statement.** This kind of statement is usually intended to spark or trigger reflective thought about a teacher decision that was observed and noticed. "Mr. Jones I was impressed with your student's answers to their bell ringers". To follow this reflective statement the administrator should follow up with a **Reflective Question:** "Is tracking their bell ringers and exit ticket data helping to drive your instruction?"

The third of the statements you can offer is a **Simple Statement.** This kind of statement is usually intended to inform the teacher that you recognized a research based strategy or approach and its effectiveness in the observed lesson, "Mrs. Ross, I noticed your students predicting, and inferring the outcome of "Romeo and Juliet". To follow this simple statement the administrator should follow up with a **Simple Question:** "Do you think that most will draw the right conclusions?" If you recollect this reading strategy is #15 on page 94. This means **your principal noticed** that you were utilizing an effective strategy for teaching on the famous Shakespearean work of Romeo and Juliet.

An effective administrator would also indorse, in a simple statement or question, that to make "Romeo and Juliet" relevant and build a bridge of contemporization with today's students, this teacher should consider doing a "Compare Contrast" analysis to the musical, "West Side Story". What strategy(s) would this recommendation speak to from pages 93-94? Would this be a good reference(s)? Why? Why not?

Chapter 18

What does

that make me?

In years past, first year teachers were considered rookies in education and required to be paired with a seasoned teacher to support them through their first year. This of course assuming that new educators lacked the experience and the know how to not only manage their classrooms but also were deficient in practices to effectively teach. I am not too convinced that this is the case anymore since we now live in this vast world of technology.

Most new teachers transport a breath of fresh air to the profession because of their experiences with social media and technology. Such huge and significant gains in technology bring a newfangled perspective to resource tools thus making teaching **more connected with what children can do** with electronics. Just ten years ago I-Phones, tablets, laptops, notepads, and other "educational" gadgets did not exist. Now that they do new teachers appear to be more prepared to use them. Therefore I believe it's more beneficial for seasoned teachers to be balanced with a millennial educator because it makes for working smarter not harder.

With that understood Carolyn Downey recognized the three types of educators that can be celebrated by conducting walkthroughs. One is not superior to the other nor is one worse than the other.

The goalmouth is to identify what "type" of educators are teaching our children and what approaches **SHOULD be taken** when giving criticism or when aiding them when challenges or desires to improve their pedagogy arise.

The first style of teacher that can be identified during first quarter walkthroughs is the **Dependent** teacher. When preparing for a walkthrough follow up, the dependent educator may require a:

❖ **Direct conversation**. The administrator should be prepared to provide direct feedback to the teacher. The administrator directly gives feedback in the conversation at hand. Administrators who are well informed on those aforementioned Marzano 9 strategies should recommend the one (or two) that would best suit the issue at hand.

The second style of teacher that can be identified during first quarter walkthroughs is the **Independent** teacher. When preparing for walkthrough follow up, the independent educator may require an:

❖ **Indirect conversation**. The administrator should invite the teacher to reflect on the short segment of noted teaching. Then, follow up on those teaching practices *that the teacher brings up*, and finish with a reflective question. This will trigger the teacher to come up with the teaching strategy that best fits the issue at hand.

The third style of teacher that can be identified during first quarter walkthroughs is the **Interdependent** teacher. When preparing for walkthrough follow up, the interdependent educator may require a:

❖ **Collegial conversation.** This educator obviously understands their strategies, why they is using them, and can identify why that practice was chosen in the noted lesson. The administrator poses a reflective question in the conversation and engages in further dialogue in the near future with the teacher.

Walkthroughs are short focused-informal observations that will help administrators and teachers **expose or highlight** a possible area of reflection. Walkthroughs should continually be conducted with a curriculum and instructional aim **never as punitive or evaluative emphasis**. Walkthroughs should foster follow up feedback with one of three types of conversations. Those conversations should include a statement and a question. This protocol, if executed faithfully on a daily basis will establish an informal and collaborative culture between teachers and administrators.

Walkthroughs have grave implications on an administrator being the victim of a dog and pony show. Do you know how I could tell the teachers in my new building were not used to administrators in their classrooms? Every time I walked in I could sense nervousness, urgency and a need to impress me. This was not good. I had to change that mindset.

The only way to amend that threatening culture was to conduct so many walkthroughs that teachers and students became **desensitized to my presence**. Two months into the year, students and teachers viewed my visits as normal, and made me feel as if I was part of the class.

Being afraid of the principal was not who I wanted to be. Fear is a **temporary emotion** and I understood the ramifications of becoming feared. My objective was to evolve into the three pronged principal; respected as **the instructional leader** of the building, effective in the **managing of humans**, and **approachable** to teachers, students and parents. I knew this to be effective leadership because it was how I felt about Mr. Martin, Dr. Robinson, and Mrs. Nickerson; all great educational leaders and mentors I was blessed to work with and for.

The definitive aim in this protocol of feedback is to **always** be engaged in learning and teaching as the instructional leader of your building. I recall when student, parent, and adult issues hindered me from my walkthroughs of classrooms. So what I decided needed to be done was to set certain blocks of time devoted to walkthroughs. I made certain to inform my executive assistant that other than for a dire excuse such as a fire, earthquake, or the second coming, I was not to be interrupted or disturbed during "walkthrough time".

After a month or so, I fashioned an environment where that set time meant I was "unavailable". It had to wait! Visiting my teachers and students were priorities that established these outcomes:

- A Positive School Culture; established!
- Education; valued!
- Together we moved away from "The way things have always been done".
- Together we moved away from traditional, convenient and simple.
- Together we moved toward meaningful, effective and useful learning practices.

The inferences of a walkthrough on teaching, learning, school climate, and school culture are felt, seen and heard in every corner of the facility! As you the teacher, or the administrator, commit to taking a daily dose of **PerCoDiff** and agree to live by "**Every Child Is Worthy and Safe**", your students and stakeholders will begin to reach across the aisle and re-program their thinking; I promise.

Chapter 19
Renewing of
the minds

What is the primary target in all of this? Hopefully for you, like me, was to take a failing or struggling community to another level, a place where failure is not an option, a facility where human beings are not okay with mediocrity, and **resignation.** One of the most dangerous and pathetic behaviors in struggling schools is to accept abnormality and dysfunction as the norm.

Administrators and teachers must have the **moral courage and courageous leadership** to talk about the elephant in the room and begin to plan to improve the climate and culture of a setting where humans reside for hours, days, weeks, and months at a time.

It takes a brave soul whether administrator or teacher to admit that change is needed. To be **resilient means** to self-reflect, to analyze, and to gage whether **teaching is actually reaching the students and if leadership is reaching teachers** for the betterment of the school. Everyone involved has to agree that change is required.

For this to manifest and come to fruition **likeminded educators have to accept** that it is utter lunacy, craziness, and impossible to continue doing what has always been done and anticipate a different outcome.

Teaching can only reach students if teachers **and** administrators are active members, invested members, believers and cheerleaders of young people despite their shortcomings and the baggage they come with!

Personality and passion are one and the same and not mutually exclusive of one another. One cannot exist without the other. Risks have to be taken even if it means that an idea or practice failed. **Replacing** negativity with the possibility that things can change for the better is the first hurdle of educating young minds.

All too often I have seen great teachers, full of outstanding knowledge, but have no relationship skills set to deal with urban children. Additionally, and unfortunately I have had the displeasure of working for leaders who are efficient data analyst and great with the disaggregation of numbers and percentages but feel that replying good morning to custodians or secretaries is beneath their dignity. No leadership position gives anyone the right to mistreat, or regard others as if they are inferior due to **the supposed power** they possess.

A valuable leader understands that authority and position are a blessing from above and that holding that position requires you to be a good custodian of power. To that end, the lone way to be prosperous is to value the teachers you have working for you, under your leadership covering, and remind them daily that without them, change is impossible. From a cheerleader's point of view **reconnecting** teachers and students with school pride, mascot pride, and school colors are the best ways to begin that metamorphosis, (in my humblest opinion!).

As mentioned in the beginning of my book, I cheered in high school, in college I was "Tuffy" the Eagle for a few seasons, and in my professional life I coached cheerleaders. My achievements as leader, teacher, and coach was built on the principles that "**being proud**" about being a Collinwood Railroader, Southview Saint, Buhrer Bulldog, Walton Wildcat, and now a Mighty Golden Scared Scarab, was paramount in shifting the mental state of humans walking through the threshold doorway(s) of my facility.

Research your mascot! Extrapolate those characteristics your mascot possess and make them come alive. When I first stepped into East Tech, I was shocked at the lack of pride the students had for their Scarab and their colors. It was sad and rather shocking because if you know anything about East Tech, you know that it used to be unbeatable in Basketball, and track. I was amazed and saddened that no one had created school spirit on the premise that East Tech was the home of **World Champions Jesse Owens and Harrison Dillard.**

In 2010 when asked to take over the cheer team which had been out of commission for several years, Mrs. Nickerson stated, "I remember what you did at Collinwood with the cheer team, think you can do that here?" It was a huge undertaking even for me due to all the negative murmuring I heard in the hallways. It was ruthless enough the children in the district referred to the Scarab mascot as a cockroach and its colors as "dooky brown and piss yellow", but to hear our own students mocking and down grading it as well was appalling. How was I ever going to turn this culture around?

It seemed an impossible project to **reconnect** the new Scarab millennials to that of the old, pride filled, championship days, of Scarab Nation. In order to generate some enthusiasm, I had to lay down the foundations to what it really meant to be a Scarab. I researched this small creature and discovered these interesting facts:

In Ancient times, the Egyptians were captivated by the **resilience** of the Sacred Scarab. They observed its **tenacity** in the harshest conditions of the hot desert as it was the only living creature able to **withstand** the desert heat and wind. The Ancient Egyptians recorded and observed the scarab's capability to **bear** 100 times its body weight as it elevated food and other objects over long distances. They marveled at the Sacred Scarab's skill to conceal itself in the desert floor giving the illusion of disappearing forever in the sand dunes only to witness days later, the Scarab emerging from the depths of the earth not as one but as hundreds. There was a belief that the Sacred Scarab had **regenerative powers** not only to return from the dead, but also to **resurrect** itself in great numbers! The Ancient Egyptians deemed the Sacred Scarab the Deity Ra whom was charged with **rolling the sun across the sky out** of the darkness and into the light.

Talk about pride and how to use this brief history as a basis for **resurrecting** Scarab Pride? This paragraph would soon change the entire dynamics of East Tech if I had anything to do with it. Knowing the plights my students face every day in this community, this was a perfect vehicle to reconnect our entire community of Scarabs to what it really means to be an East Tech Mighty Sacred Golden Scarab!

This passage was shared with every coach, and every athlete in the building. It was a portion of initiation into athletic teams and clubs and was made common knowledge in Freshmen English. Beginning with the cheer team, it stood at the forefront of bringing back to life what had been shut down, dormant and eradicated throughout the past twenty years in the East Tech community.

At senior parent and freshmen initiation night in early September, another function and tradition I shaped, this event set the tone for those new to our legacy and those on the verge of departing from it. What a great way to begin and end a school year!

Since then, this has been the mantra of East Tech students; **when we are faced with challenges and tribulations and suppose we cannot lever the heat of our existential plights, we discover ways "to roll out" of the encounters of life and create new existence, new hope, and new vision. This is what Mighty Sacred Golden Scarabs do; Roll out from the old and formulate new verve out of tough dilemmas.**

Every departing senior marching across the commencement stage, (another project I am charged with), knows when he experiences the ordeals and distresses of life, feels trapped, unable to escape the harsh tasks of life, or can't weather the heat in his own personal storm of life; he is reminded he is a Mighty Sacred Golden Scarab!. Our seniors are encouraged to have hope for a fresh new existence ahead!   They are reminded of the rich history and ancient legacy of Resilience, Tenacity, Regeneration, Emergence, Strength,

Honor, and Power that they come from. Every graduate knows that from that day forward, they will always be, forever be A Scarab, a Mighty Sacred Golden East Tech Scarab!

Last year a former student came to visit me at East Tech and confessed how she was financially struggling in college. She was on the verge of dropping out. Rather than to give up and surrender, she pulled out her graduation program where this history of the Scarab was written. She told me that failure was out of the question and because she *is a Scarab,* she located and discovered some resources that helped her to remain in school and press forward toward earning her degree in Nursing. This student not only defied the odds, she did it with character, integrity, and with the pride of being a successful Scarab for life! Wow!

What a difference it makes to **reduce distracting** behaviors or accepting the vicious cycle of remaining captive to "hood life". Noshala did not accept financial challenges as a reason to throw in the towel; she understood that her only mission was to press upward and onward from a dark situation into the light of possibilities.

All of your participants will enjoy this shift. This phenomenon of change in climate, attitude, mindset, school pride, and academic transformation, of all your stakeholders, will witness student achievement and your school's report card go from:

Resignation to Resilience:

- **By Replacing** negative attitudes about learning with productive perspectives about the role of risk-taking (and even failure) as a necessary and purposeful part of the learning process.

- **By Reconnecting** with School Pride, with learning, and with a belief in students as competent learners who are capable, valued, and respected.

- **By Rebuilding** life skills and learning skills that lead to academic success and also lay the groundwork for success in life.

- **By Reducing** the need to use unproductive and distracting behaviors as a means of self-protection.

Teachers and administrators have no business in education if they do not possess the skill set to deal with people; all people, young people, teaching people, maintenance people, clerical people, people with little knowledge and people who possess an abundance of knowledge, people of like skin color and people whose pigmentation doesn't resemble their own!

I have been blessed to work with great disciplinarians who have met and exceeded the skill set to manage staff and students, but abuse their power to be-little, de-humanize, de-fame, emasculate, and embarrass children, parents and fellow educators. All of which negate the great skills they possess.

117

No one wants to work in a facility where they dread driving to every morning no matter how great or challenging the community is there.

Unfortunately some leaders whom I've worked with were under the belief that in order to increase (in salary and position) they had to decrease others by knit-picking their evaluations, involuntarily transferring them, or making life so miserable for them that they either quit the profession or requested a transfer to another facility.

There are ways to deal with nay-Sayers and folks that push back on your teaching and leading philosophy without compromising your integrity, character, or the Christ **that hopefully** lives in you. If promotion is decreed in the eternal plan for your life, no devil in hell can stop what God has ordained for you. There is no need for any leader or teacher to destroy or attempt to destroy someone else's livelihood or bully humans to buy into your belief system, style of leading, and style of teaching.   If it's meant to be it will manifest. God knows exactly what he is doing, and where to place you in the world to make HIS purpose in you work for the betterment of children and teachers.

This entire manual has been a two decade work in progress created with the sole intention to aid new educators and refresh the mind of seasoned educators. Being blessed to have taught at all three levels of education and be an administrator at all three level has given me the maximum benefits to create this resource guide for educators.

The walkthrough process will yield maximum benefits only if a carefully structured method for sharing the data is established. Teachers and administrators will quickly learn that individual classrooms and the entire facility *will* operate more effectively in this **new** context of cultural/climate expectations, if implemented and done with fidelity. The old **has to be buried** along with its common notion about "the ways things have always been done here" which may have developed over the years eventually deteriorating the leading and teaching due to traditional, convenient and simple practices which have not been meaningful, effective, or for that matter, useful!

In Cleveland, teachers are evaluated as ineffective, developing, skilled, or accomplished. We have to accept these implications as obvious and accept that each will require some individual attention. It is, therefore, incumbent upon any administrator to challenge the culture of his building using this manual as a guideline, and as **a basis for change**.

My prayer is that my years of experiences both worthy and unscrupulous have helped produce this tool to help you **unearth a "way in"** to eradicate the negative commonly held expectations and practices in your school. I sense my recommendations will shine a bright light everywhere, so long as you implement and practice them diligently and vigilantly.

Professional growth will only happen in an atmosphere when everyone takes their daily dose of **PerCoDiff** and live by **Every Child Is Worthy & Safe**.

If this guide is formulaic in its attention to specific information gathering, it becomes far less formulaic in its application of the information toward the goal of creating an exemplary place of learning. In fact, as for my own personal and professional experiences, the construction of this book has led me to inquiry, interpretation, and research into effective practices that work for and with urban children and educators.

To close, I would like to express the importance of training and convincing all members of the facility you work in to get on board and on the same page from administrators, teachers, paraprofessionals, assistants, tutors, to counselors, parents and guardians; all stakeholders! This resource tool should not be secretive or evaluative in nature. With stakeholders **"all in"**, professional growth can be identified and explored in a variety of interdependent settings. Patterns and commonalities can be shared in whole-building contexts, with development of grade-level teams, departments, and individual teachers whom are charged with **building bridges of efficacy** in education that connect ALL sides to learning and mastery.

It is with my heartfelt hope this tool will not only aid you in the leading of teachers and the teaching of young minds, but will also benefit you to better educate, lead, and empower yourself toward being the preeminent educationalist of humans.

References:

- Carolyn Downey. The Three-Minute Classroom Walk-Through.
- Robert Marzano. Classroom Instruction that Works.
- Common Core State Standards. Quick Flip Reference www.edupress.com.
- Kathleen Cleveland. ...Resignation to Resilience. HSTW presenter 2011 Conference. teacherOnlineEducation.com
- Barbara Fowler. Critical Thinking Across the Curriculum.
- Gregory & Kuzmich. Differentiated Learning Strategies.
- Forget 2004
- Elder and Paul 2003
- Silver, Strong, Perini 2007 The Strategic Teacher
- Myra Cloer Reynolds. Ten Strategies for Creating a Classroom Culture of High Expectations.
- The Leadership and Learning Center. Navigating the Common Core Standards. (Book One/Book Two.

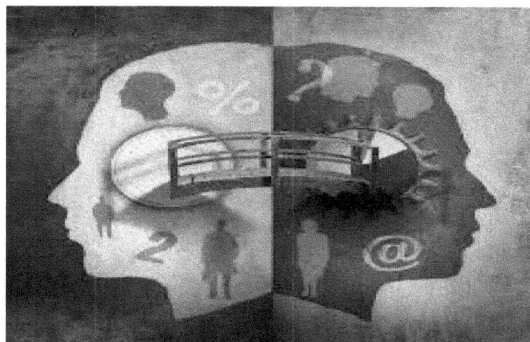